# Great Botanic Gardens
## OF THE WORLD

**Sara Oldfield**

**BGCI**
*Plants for the Planet*

NEW HOLLAND

First published in 2007 by New Holland Publishers (UK) Ltd
London • Cape Town • Sydney • Auckland

www.newhollandpublishers.com

Garfield House, 86–88 Edgware Road, London W2 2EA,
United Kingdom

80 McKenzie Street, Cape Town 8001, South Africa

Unit 1, 66 Gibbes Street, Chatswood, NSW 2067, Australia

218 Lake Road, Northcote, Auckland, New Zealand

ISBN 978 1 84537 593 5

Editorial Director: Jo Hemmings
Senior Editor: James Parry
Design: Gülen Shevki-Taylor, Adam Morris and Alan Marshall
Production: Joan Woodroffe

Reproduction by Pica Digital Pte Ltd, Singapore
Printed and bound in Singapore by Tien Wah Press (Pte) Ltd

front cover: The Japanese Garden at the Huntington Botanical
Gardens, California, USA (photo: The Huntington Library, Art
Collections and Botanical Gardens © The Huntington); front
flap: Handkerchief Tree (photo: Howard Rice); back cover:
Marimutra Botanic Garden, Blanes, Spain (photo: BGCI);
page 1: The Japanese Garden at Missouri Botanical Garden,
USA (photo: Missouri Botanical Garden); page 2: The limestone
rock garden, looking towards the glasshouse, at the University
Botanic Garden in Cambridge, England.
right: Plants on display in the Orchid House at Durban
Botanical Gardens, South Africa.
page 6, left to right: Cycad (BGCI); Orchid (Magnus Lidén);
Water-lilies (Fairchild Tropical Botanic Garden); Polyanthus
(Robert Benson/NYBG).

# CONTENTS

CLARENCE HOUSE

Botanic gardens play a unique role in connecting people and plants. They inspire us by providing stunning visual displays of plants that are often rare in cultivation; they provide living laboratories for botanical research and, increasingly, they are vital in conserving plant species that are under threat in the wild. I am particularly proud of my patronage of the Foundation and Friends of the Royal Botanic Gardens at Kew, and of the Royal Botanic Gardens in Edinburgh, both of which I enjoy visiting enormously – not least because they provide practical ideas for my own garden!

I am delighted that this new book, published in association with another of my patronages, Botanic Gardens Conservation International (B.G.C.I.), encourages wide appreciation of botanic gardens highlighting their architectural, historical, horticultural and landscape treasures – and the important green spaces they provide in city areas. Botanic gardens exist in most countries of the world, ranging from the splendid formal gardens with manicured lawns and impressive glasshouses, to small community gardens growing local plants. All have their role to play in promoting the value of plants.

The crucially important conservation role of botanic gardens is strongly emphasized within the book. Over 30 per cent of the world's known plants are grown in botanic gardens, including at least 9,000 which are threatened with extinction in the wild. The knowledge and skills of botanic garden staff help secure valuable plant resources for human well-being, particularly in poorer countries which, for example, depend on wild plants for 80 per cent of their medicines. I am, therefore, enormously encouraged that royalties from the sale of this book will contribute to B.G.C.I.'s work to ensure that 90 per cent of the world's most endangered plant species are conserved – a target of the internationally-agreed "Global Strategy for Plant Conservation". To do this, B.G.C.I. will draw on the skills and expertize of botanic gardens around the world to conserve endangered plants, both within the gardens and in their natural environments. Special emphasis will be given to plants for health and nutrition.

I hope that this remarkable book will be enjoyed by active and armchair gardeners and botanists, members of horticultural societies and, above all, the many visitors to botanic gardens worldwide.

# Chapter 1

# THE DIVERSITY OF
# BOTANIC GARDENS

Creating gardens is a universal pursuit. Growing

plants for food, pleasure, medicine, fuel and shelter

takes place everywhere that people live. Botanic gardens

are a special category of garden, distinctive for their

scientific basis, inspirational planting, commitment

to plant conservation and involvement in

environmental education.

A botanic garden can be defined as "An institution holding documented collections of living plants for the purposes of scientific research, conservation, display and education". Today there are over 2000 botanic gardens around the world, providing an opportunity for study and enjoyment for all. This global botanic garden network also provides a tremendous resource for the conservation and sustainable use of the world's increasingly threatened flora.

# GARDENS FROM EARLY HISTORY

The first gardens, cultivating plants with economic or ornamental value, were created in Egypt, Assyria, China and Mexico. One of the earliest gardens of which any records remain is the Royal Garden of Tutmosis III, created around 3,000 years ago. Attached to the Temple of Karnak in ancient Egypt, this garden featured rows of cultivated palms, a vine pergola and pools with lotus plants. Also in ancient times, the Assyrians and Babylonians planted wooded parks, partly for hunting but also for aesthetic reasons.

Pleasure gardens are known to have existed in China for thousands of years, and from early times the Chinese people cultivated flowers and appreciated their beauty. Around 3000 BC, the legendary Emperor Shen Nung composed the Pen T'sao Ching, which documented the impressive total of 365 different herbal remedies. Ginseng was used medicinally at that time, together with opium and ephedra, and Shen Nung's collection of plants can be considered a very early form of botanic garden.

While Chinese gardens were very stylized and represented idealized landscapes, Japanese gardens, which date from around 1,700 years ago, were more abstract, with strong symbolic elements. Both the Chinese and Japanese regarded their gardens as domestic interpretations of the vast untamed nature beyond the garden boundaries.

The ancient Mexicans also held nature in high esteem. The emperors created gardens with a range of plants from throughout the mountain and forest regions of the country, establishing medicinal plant collections at gardens such as those of Montezuma. Most of these gardens were destroyed during the Spanish conquest, but the famous pre-Hispanic garden of Chapultepec survived until recent times in what is now a major park in Mexico City.

In Europe, the Romans created various forms of beautiful garden, although these were invariably formal in design and often located within the courtyards of villas. Garden flowerbeds were used to display a range of herbaceous plants, with popular species at the time including irises, hyacinths, pansies, narcissi, anemones, carnations, foxgloves, jasmine and roses.

The Romans also cultivated a wide range of herbs and medicinal plants, and took many of their favourites with them to the furthermost corners of their enormous empire. Garden water features were also highly popular and ranged from tranquil pools to elaborate fountains. Beyond the immediate villa garden, plane trees were planted as avenues, and cypress trees were widely used to create structure and decorative effect. Indeed, it has been said that until the fall of the Roman Empire, the whole of Italy resembled a garden. However, during the period that followed, gardens throughout Europe fell into general disrepair, with the formal garden tradition surviving only within monasteries.

Monastic gardens were developed mainly to supply the needs of the monastic community, namely fresh fruit and vegetables, herbs, medicinal plants and flowers for the altar and shrines. However, these gardens were designed to be beautiful as well as functional, with gardening considered to be an activity that could calm a troubled soul. More than this, gardens took on a greater

Meridies

Septentrio

significance for those Christian thinkers who believed that gardening was a way of recreating the paradise which man had once shared with God. Commonly grown devotional plants included the lily and the rose.

A plan of the monastery of St Gall in Switzerland, which dates from the ninth century, shows a formal garden layout with rectangular beds separated by narrow paths. This was the typical design and the basis of the monastic gardening tradition that arrived in England with the Norman conquest of 1066. This heritage had a strong influence on Medieval gardens, in part recognizing the value of plants as a source of scientific knowledge. Medieval gardens were commonly enclosed and continued to grow plants for medicine, food and pleasure. Species of iris, periwinkle, marigold and peony were well-established in cultivation.

## THE INFLUENCE OF THE RENAISSANCE

Botanic gardens as we know them today date from the 16th century. Originally, the gardens had a strong emphasis on the growth and study of medicinal plants, most drugs at the time being derived from plants, and it was not until the late 19th century that medicine and botany evolved as separate disciplines. Botanic or physic gardens were needed to train medical practitioners in the identification and use of different plant species, maintaining a tradition established in the earliest times. By the 14th century university gardens for apothecaries were established in cities like Prague and Cologne, but it was in Italy that the first Renaissance university gardens were established.

The first true botanic garden was established in Italy in 1543, at the University of Pisa, and laid out by Luca

PAGE 8: Lush vegetation including tree ferns at Kadoorie Farm and Botanic Garden in Hong Kong.

ABOVE: This view of a formal Dutch flower garden comes from one of the most famous of early gardening books, *Hortus Floridus*, engraved by Crispin van de Pass.

Photo: Fiona Wild

ABOVE: The Botanic Garden at Padua is one of the oldest in the world and is a World Heritage Site.

OPPOSITE TOP: Oxford Botanic Garden viewed from Magdalen College Tower. The garden is still important for teaching university undergraduates, thereby continuing a centuries-old tradition.

OPPOSITE BOTTOM: Vegetables at the Oxford Botanic Garden. The garden has a strong commitment to promoting sustainability. There is currently a resurgence of interest in home vegetable growing in the UK and the Oxford vegetable beds demonstrate what can be achieved.

Ghini, next to the Medici Arsenal on the right bank of the river Arno, close to an old monastery. Luca Ghini was Professor of Medicine at Bologna, when the Grand Duke Cosimo I de'Medici of Tuscany called him to Pisa to teach botany. Ghini immediately realized the need for a garden to demonstrate live plants to his students, together with a collection of dried plants in a herbarium, and accurate botanical drawings. With Ghini's historic development of a herbarium, the future of the study of botany took a decisive step forwards: not only could plants be studied in the garden, they could also be dried and pressed and examined at leisure. Many famous naturalists and scientists came to visit the new garden in Pisa, with its beds of poisonous plants, prickly plants, aromatic plants and wetland species. When the Arsenal was enlarged in 1563, the gardens had to be moved. The second garden was created by Andrea Cesalpino, a great botanist, scientist and doctor, thought to be the first person to study plants for their own sake rather than for medical, decorative or magical reasons. Cesalpino gave his name to the plant genus Caesalpinia, which includes the national tree of Brazil, *Caesalpinia echinata*, a commercially valuable source of red dye from the days

of the early colonial settlement of Brazil. The final version of the botanic garden at Pisa, the University Botanical Gardens, was created between 1591 and 1592 and remains at the same site today.

The Universities of Florence and Padua soon followed the example set at Pisa, and created their own botanic gardens in 1545. Rome established its garden in around 1566, and Bologna in 1567. The Orto Botanico in Padua, northern Italy, was devoted to medicinal plants. It is still at its original site in the centre of the city and retains its original circular design. Within the wall, the garden is laid out in small beds with stone edgings, a geometrical layout that remained fashionable in garden design into the 17th century. Until 1984, the oldest plant in the garden was an example of *Vitex agnus-castus* (known as Chasteberry, and used to treat women's hormonal disturbances and also as a pepper substitute), documented since 1550. Since the demise of this specimen, the oldest plant has been a palm, *Chamaerops humilis* var. *arborescens*, which has been on the site since 1585. The global importance of the botanic garden in Padua was formally acknowledged in 1997, when it was declared a World Heritage Site, in recognition that "the garden was the starting point for botanic gardens in the world and represents the cradle of science, scientific exchange and the relationship between nature and culture. It has contributed greatly to the development of many modern scientific disciplines, notably botany, medicine, chemistry, ecology and pharmacy".

By the end of the 16th century there were botanical gardens at Kassel, Leipzig, Breslau, Leiden, Heidelberg and Montpellier, each with a herbarium. The botanic garden in Leiden, in the Netherlands, dates back to 1587. Under the direction of Carolus Clusius, by 1601 this garden was growing nearly a thousand different plant species, including tropical plants such as sugarcane, ginger and other 'exotics' such as potato, maize, tomato, peppers and prickly pear.

The oldest botanic garden in the UK is the Oxford Botanic Garden, established with a donation of £5,000 by Sir Henry Danvers, the Earl of Danby, who wished the garden to be established for "the glorification of God and for the furtherance of learning". The gardens were finished in 1633 and the first curator, Jacob Bobart, was appointed in 1642. When he first came to the garden he generated an income by selling fruit, such as the Medlar, *Mespilus germanica*, grown within the garden walls. The oldest tree that can be seen in the Oxford Botanic Garden today is an English Yew, planted by Bobart in 1645.

Photo: Oxford University Botanic Garden

VEGETABLES

Photo: Oxford University Botanic Garden

# COLLECTION AND CLASSIFICATION

The creation of botanic gardens in the 16th century coincided with a time of global exploration and major advances in plant discovery. Over the following centuries botanic gardens became associated with the development of tropical agriculture and colonial expansion. The Royal Botanic Garden in Madrid, for example, following its founding in 1755, promoted many botanical expeditions to the Americas, and the Botanic Garden of La Orotava, Tenerife, was established in 1788 to acclimatize new and potentially useful plants from the New World.

The growing interest in collecting plants from around the world led to a need for a standard way of classifying and naming species. There were various attempts to do this but the enduring method, which has allowed the systematic development of plant taxonomy, was devised by the Swedish botanist Carolus Linnaeus, who ran the Uppsala Botanic Garden (which had been established in 1644 by Olof Rudbeck, a professor of medicine) from 1741 until his death in 1778. During his time as director, Linnaeus obtained plants from all over the world, mainly as herbarium specimens but also for the garden, which he restored following a period of neglect. The Uppsala Botanic Garden is Sweden's oldest, and the original construction and layout can still be seen today, together with many of the species that were grown in the time of Linnaeus. The oldest plants include four 250-year-old specimens of Linnaeus's Laurels.

Today the Uppsala Botanic Garden extends over nearly 14 hectares, growing around 11,000 species and cultivars from all over the world. The garden is divided into different sections: economic plants, rock and arid gardens, stone troughs, peat beds, annual beds and areas for research and education. There is also a Tropical Greenhouse, which grows about 4,000 species. The garden provides plant material and horticultural support for research and education within Uppsala University, which tutors over a thousand students each year in botany, pharmacology, horticulture or ecology. It also seeks to improve public awareness of all aspects of biodiversity. The country home of Linnaeus can still be seen a short distance from Uppsala at Hammarby, where the farmhouse and garden he bought in 1758 are preserved as a monument to the founder of modern botany.

Photo: The Linnean Society

ABOVE: Born in 1707, Linnaeus has been described variously as the 'King of Flowers', the father of botany, and the world's first ecologist.

RIGHT: Uppsala Botanic Garden was formerly attached to a royal palace. It has played an important role in educating people about plants for over 300 years.

Photo: Magnus Lidén

# GARDENS AND THE AGE OF DISCOVERY

The Royal Botanic Gardens, Kew, was established in the 18th century and rose to scientific eminence with the appointment of Joseph Banks as Scientific Adviser in 1772. The gardens at Kew were instrumental in the development of plantation crops such as rubber and quinine, and played a decisive role in breaking the Dutch monopoly on the Asian spice trade by introducing spice cultivation into the Caribbean. In the early 18th century prizes and awards were given by the Royal Society for the introduction, establishment and dissemination of highly prized tropical species.

A botanic garden was established on St Vincent in the Caribbean in 1764, one year after the island became a British colony. General Robert Melville, then Governor of the Windward Islands, was responsible for creating the garden, for "the cultivation and improvement of many plants now growing wild and the import of others from similar climates" which "would be of great utility to the public and vastly improve the resources of the island". In 1783 Dr Alexander Anderson became curator of the garden, working closely with Sir Joseph Banks to acquire new plants for his Caribbean garden. In 1791 nutmeg and black pepper were introduced from French Guiana, and Anderson was also responsible for the introduction of the fruits *Syzygium malaccensis*, the Plum Rose or Malay Apple, and *Averrhoa carambola*, the Carambola or Star Fruit.

Captain William Bligh was heading for St Vincent in the Bounty with a cargo of Breadfruit Trees, *Artocarpus altilis,* when the famous mutiny broke out in 1789. The Kew botanist on the epic voyage, David Nelson, remained loyal to Bligh but ultimately perished on Java after being cast adrift by the mutineers. Despite this famous setback, Bligh returned undaunted to Tahiti on the HMS *Providence* and completed his mission to St Vincent in January 1793. Anderson took great care of the newly arrived plants, and the success of both expedition and plant introduction is evident in the wide distribution of breadfruit, now a useful, high-energy food plant throughout the Caribbean. Among the wide variety of tropical trees and shrubs that grow in the St Vincent garden today is a third-generation Breadfruit Tree, a sucker from the original plant brought by Captain Bligh.

Another early tropical botanic garden was established at Pamplemousses, Mauritius, in 1735 by Governor Mahé de Labourdonnais, who founded the island's sugar industry. Initially food crops and other useful plants were the main species grown by the garden, which developed into an important supplier of fresh food for ships calling at Port Louis. Ornamental horticulture was introduced to the garden in 1772.

One of the most notorious stories of early tropical agriculture relates to the establishment of the rubber industry. Sir Joseph Hooker, Director of Kew from 1865 to 1885, arranged for seeds of the Brazilian Rubber Tree, *Hevea brasiliensis*, to be collected in Brazil against the wishes of the local governor. Permission was granted for Henry Wickham to take the seeds out of the country in 1876, under the pretence that these were a gift for Queen Victoria. Seedlings of the rubber plant, produced at Kew, were then sent to the Botanic Garden at Henaratgoda, Sri Lanka and later to the Singapore Botanic Garden. With advice from Kew, plantations were soon developed in the Far East, and the great rubber boom of 1910 made Malaya the most successful rubber-producing country of the time, thanks largely to H.N. Ridley, director of Singapore Botanic Garden.

A botanic garden was established in Calcutta in 1787 by Robert Kyd, with advice from Joseph Banks, and the garden remains on the same site today, on the banks of the Hooghly. At that time Calcutta was enjoying a period of great prosperity as a centre of trading for the East India Company. The initial emphasis was on the acclimatization of teak, which it was hoped would provide a source of timber to replace the dwindling supply of oak for the East India Company's shipyard at Deptford, in London. Agricultural research was also important; the Calcutta garden helped to establish tea cultivation in India, and introduced mahogany, sugar-cane and jute. The garden later developed as an attractive recreational site for the growing city; paths, vistas and water features were developed and a wide variety of ornamental trees was planted. With the cooperation of Kew, the Calcutta garden introduced quinine from South America to India. Quinine originated from the bark of *Cinchona* trees native to the Andes. It was first known in Europe in the 17th century in the form of ground bark, introduced by the Jesuits. In 1820 the alkaloid within the bark, the active medicinal ingredient, was isolated. This led to the rapid destruction of many trees within the Andean forests, but by the 1860s plant collectors from Kew had obtained sufficient material for the development of Cinchona cultivation in Calcutta and elsewhere, and the Dutch were also working hard to establish Cinchona cultivation in their own colonies. The success of the garden in Calcutta helped to inspire the development of botanic gardens in Bogor, Indonesia, in 1817; Peradeniya, Ceylon (now Sri Lanka), in 1821; and Singapore in 1859.

## THE PASSION FOR ORNAMENTAL PLANTS

Alongside the development of new commercial crops in the 16th to 19th centuries there was a growing interest in new ornamental plants. Clusius, the early director of Leiden Botanic Garden, helped to popularize the tulip, which was first introduced from Turkey to Vienna in 1554. Clusius received some of the first seeds when he was working as prefect of the Royal Medicinal Garden, Prague, and continued his interest when he moved to Leiden. He is credited with helping to launch the Dutch bulb industry. The huge European interest in growing tulips, 'tulipmania', reached its peak in the 1630s, with bulbs changing hands for hundreds of pounds each. However, supply soon began to exceed demand, tulips ceased to be so rare, and prices fell accordingly. By 1637 the bottom had fallen out of the market and those who had invested at its peak lost heavily, often going bankrupt.

The heyday of collection of new ornamental plants for cultivation was the Victorian era, extending into the early years of the 20th century. One of the most spectacular plants, still to be seen in many botanic gardens today, is the Giant Water-lily, *Victoria amazonica*, a species native to South America, and the national flower of Guyana. Commissioned by the British Government to delineate the boundaries of British Guiana, Robert Schomburgk was one of the first Europeans to see *Victoria*, whilst travelling there in 1837. He collected material which was used to describe the genus. The discovery of the Giant Water-lily caused much excitement in London and the plant was named after the new Queen. Kew received

seeds from South America in 1849 and Joseph Paxton, head of the gardens at Chatsworth House in Derbyshire, was the first to produce flowering plants of the water-lily in cultivation. Giant Water-lilies are displayed in many gardens today. The Adelaide Botanic Garden in Australia has long been associated with this magnificent plant, as

Richard Schomburgk, brother of Robert, was the second director of the garden. *Victoria amazonica* first flowered in the Victoria House at the Adelaide Botanic Garden in 1868, again causing huge public interest. The delightful Waterlily House at Kew, constructed in 1852, was originally intended for the display of *Victoria*, but now grows tropical *Nymphaea* water-lilies and the Sacred Lotus, *Nelumbo lucifera*, which has been grown at Kew since its introduction to the gardens by Sir Joseph Banks in 1784.

Exotic orchids have been cultivated in Europe since the 17th century, but it was not until the 19th century

Giant Water-lilies (*Victoria amazonica*) are a popular feature of botanic gardens worldwide.

Photo: BGCI

Photo: Magnus Lidén

A particularly stunning orchid, *Paphiopedium rothschildianum* has attracted the interest of unscrupulous plant collectors in the past. It is currently listed as 'Endangered' in the wild.

that large-scale cultivation took place. The first tropical orchid to flower at Kew was *Encyclia cochleata*, an epiphytic orchid from Latin America, which flowered in the 1780s. In the Victorian era orchid growing was a major horticultural craze, especially in the UK, with enormous numbers imported from the wild amid intense professional rivalry and scant regard for conservation. Sir Joseph Hooker, whilst travelling in India, noted that *Vanda coerulea* was the rarest and most beautiful of Indian orchids. He collected large numbers, but few survived the journey back to England. Orchid collecting posed a direct threat to wild orchid species, leading for example to the near demise of the Lady's Slipper Orchid, *Cypripedium calceolus*, in the UK and the endangerment of tropical species such as the *Paphiopedilum* slipper orchids. There are only about 70 species of *Paphiopedilum* in the wild but over 12,000 horticultural hybrids have been developed from them. At

the end of the 19th century *Paphiopedilum* was the most popular genus of orchid in cultivation. The fabled *P. rothschildianum*, the most spectacular of all slipper orchids, was introduced into cultivation in 1887. The nurserymen appear to have deliberately misled their rivals about the origin of this species, claiming that it had been discovered in New Guinea. In fact, *P. rothschildianum* is endemic to Mount Kinabalu in Sabah, Malaysia. Although it has been close to extinction, efforts have been made to boost the natural population of this species with material from ex-situ collections. The popularity of *Paphiopedilum* spp. declined after the Victorian era until the discovery of a new species, *P. sukhakulii*, in Thailand in the 1960s and subsequent discoveries of species in southwest China. A resurgence of collecting pressure on wild species has contributed to the near extinction of Vietnamese species in recent years.

## SPECIAL COLLECTIONS

Orchid collections continue to be a major attraction for many visitors to botanic gardens around the world. Techniques for cultivation and propagation have developed to ensure that the needless destruction of wild plants is avoided, and many botanic gardens are now involved in the conservation and restoration of orchid species. A spectacular orchid garden can be seen at the Singapore Botanic Garden, which contains over 600,000 orchid plants, representing over 400 species and 2,000 hybrids. The outdoor orchid plantings are colour-themed to represent the four seasons of the year. In total, there are around 30,000 different species of orchid known to science and approximately 25 per cent of these are cultivated in botanic gardens.

Cacti and succulent plant collections have long been a popular feature in botanic gardens. There are around 10,000 succulent plant species within 30 different families – united by their ability to store water in specially adapted stems, leaves or roots. The largest and best-known family of succulent plants is the cactus family or Cactaceae. The bizarre growth forms and brightly-coloured flowers of cacti have attracted collectors for centuries. There are over 1000 species in the Cactaceae family, all of which are native to the Americas. Following the European discovery and colonization of the New World, cacti were introduced into cultivation in Europe in the 16th century. The English apothecary Morgan included *Melocactus* plants in his collection in 1570; he was later appointed apothecary to Queen Elizabeth I, and is credited with having introduced vanilla to Britain. Linnaeus recognized 22 species of cactus in the first edition of *Species Plantarum* in 1753. In the following century newly discovered cacti caused much excitement in the horticultural world, similar to the earlier craze for tulip novelties, and some specimens were traded for huge sums of money. The Mexican Living Rock cactus, *Ariocarpus kotschoubeyanus*, for example, was first discovered by Baron Wilhelm von Karwinsky in 1830. He found only three plants of this naturally rare and well-camouflaged cactus; one he presented to the Botanical Garden of St Petersburg, the second to his patron Prince Kotschoubey, and the third was sold to a nursery in Paris for more than its weight in gold.

Nowadays, important collections of cacti and succulents are found in botanic gardens within their natural centres of diversity, for example in Mexico, the desert areas of southwestern USA, Cuba, Madagascar, South Africa and the Canary Islands, and also as exotic greenhouse collections in botanic gardens around the world. The horticultural attraction of cacti and succulents has been one of the factors threatening the survival of these plants in the world and many species are on the brink of extinction in their natural habitats. Fortunately, botanic gardens are playing a major role in conserving these species.

Alpine plants hold a special fascination for gardeners. These small, hardy plants typically grow in the wild, in mountain regions between the tree line and permanent

Succulent collections are popular in Mediterranean Europe, as shown here at the Jardin Exotique in Monaco.

Photo: Jardin Exotique de Monaco

snowline. In botanic garden collections they can be found in rockeries or in specialized glasshouses, which can provide the controlled conditions necessary for the plants to thrive. The Royal Botanic Garden, Edinburgh has a renowned collection of alpines, with plants from mountain areas all over the world. The first rock garden was built there in 1870, was completely rebuilt three decades or so later, and now extends to nearly a hectare. The rock mounds and gullies are intersected by a scree slope, on which grow plants such as the rock jasmines, *Androsace* spp., and also by a mountain stream. Around 5,000 species are grown in the rock garden, including native Scottish alpines.

The oldest alpine garden in Europe is that at the University of Vienna Botanic Belvedere Garden in Vienna. This garden is close to the historic city centre and adjacent to the botanical garden of the University of Vienna. The alpine collection was started by Archduke Johann and his brothers Rainer and Anton and was established on its present site in 1865. It now contains around 4,700 alpine plants from all over the world, including over 300 species and cultivars of *Sempervivum*.

Carnivorous plant collections usually attract much attention within botanic gardens. There are several hundred plant species that digest insects and other small animals. These plants have been objects of fascination for centuries, arousing the interest of leading naturalists such as Charles Darwin, who published the first major work on them in 1875. The Venus Flytrap, *Dionaea muscipula*, grows naturally on the coastal plains of the North and South Carolina, USA. In 1763, this extraordinary plant was described by Arthur Dobbs, then governor of North Carolina, as "the great wonder of the vegetable kingdom".

The North Carolina Botanic Garden, a garden committed to plant conservation, has recreated the natural habitat of *Dionaea muscipula* within its grounds and in the heathy wetland the Venus Flytrap grows along with native pitcher plants *Sarracenia* spp. This natural habitat garden is burned yearly to simulate processes that are part of the endangered coastal plain pine savannas and heath areas. The garden also has five raised beds displaying numerous species of pitcher plants, sundews and butterworts, as well as decorative plants commonly found in pitcher plant bogs, such as orchids, Meadow Beauty, and the Pine Lily.

Comprehensive collections of trees provide the framework for outdoor planting in many botanic gardens of the world and some specialist gardens – arboreta – are devoted entirely to their cultivation. Some of the many arboreta around the world have their origin in the commercial development of forestry and others in the passion for trees enjoyed by wealthy individuals. The Westonbirt Arboretum, now part of the UK's National Arboretum, was established by Robert Holford in the 1820s. Owning a fine country estate was considered the height of fashion at this time and Robert Holford wanted to create a picturesque landscape with an outstanding tree collection. There was much rivalry between Holford and his neighbour, the Earl of Ducie on the nearby Tortworth Estate. Holford began planting his trees on open farmland, and when the original village of Westonbirt spoilt his view he moved it in its entirety. In what is now called the Savill Glade, shelter belts of yew, box and laurel were planted to create bays for collections of azaleas, rhododendrons, magnolias and camellias. The Acer Glade and Colour Circle, planted in 1850–1875, provided Holford with a venue for entertaining his friends to magnificent picnics, surrounded by maples, spindles, Persian Ironwood trees and Katsura trees. Robert Holford was planting at the time of major plant-collecting expeditions and he commissioned collectors to bring back trees and shrubs for Westonbirt. David Douglas, for example, a plant collector for the Horticultural Society of London, was sent to America in 1822 and collected seed and plants for the next 12 years, until he met his death in the Sandwich Islands (now known as Hawaii) at the age of 35. Douglas provided Westonbirt with seed of Monterey Pine, *Pinus radiatea*, and other trees he collected, such as Douglas Fir, *Pseudotsuga menziesii*, and the Sitka Spruce, *Picea sitchensis*. George Holford, Robert's son, shared his father's passion for trees, and together they created new drives through the semi-natural oak and hazel of Silk Wood, creating new space for the magnificent conifer plantings.

The Arboretum at Westonbirt now covers 240 hectares and contains 18,500 specimens of trees and shrubs in the collection, representing 4,000 taxa. The oldest tree at the site is a native Small-leaved Lime, *Tilia cordata*, which is around 2,000 years old. The Westonbirt collection includes over a hundred specimens of rare and threatened tree species and its primary objectives are research and conservation.

OPPOSITE: The rock garden at the Royal Botanic Garden, Edinburgh, grows around 5,000 different species. It has been cultivated at its present site for the past century.

# THE ROLES AND FUNCTIONS OF BOTANIC GARDENS

One of the original aims of botanic gardens, and of the more specialized arboreta, was to build up diverse collections of plants from around the world. Exchange of plants and sharing of plant material has long been a tradition of botanic gardens. At times the acquisition of plant material from the wild involved secrecy and subterfuge and excessive collection of some species placed direct pressure on wild populations. But such examples are rare and the heritage of botanic gardens is one of genuine commitment to plant study and cultivation for the benefit of the millions of visitors who enjoy the gardens and to the understanding of plants which are necessary for food, medicines and so much more. Now most botanic gardens have clear collection policies which determine how they collect and why. With so many plants well established in cultivation there is less need to rely on new material collected from the wild – unless there is a genuine need for such material. More care is taken in collecting, in recognition of the spirit of the Convention on Biological Diversity, the new legal controls that exist in many countries and the need to prevent excessive removal of wild material.

Many gardens concentrate on the display, interpretation and conservation of the native flora in the countries where they occur. The major conservation role of botanic gardens came to the fore around 30 years ago. The USSR Botanic Gardens Council, for example, set up a special committee for threatened plant conservation in 1974 and two international conferences on conservation were held at Kew during that decade, laying the foundations for strong international cooperation by botanic gardens in conserving the world's flora – a theme which is described in more detail in the next chapter.

## A TEACHING TRADITION

Botanic gardens in all countries help to inspire an interest in the diversity of plants both native and exotic. The formal teaching tradition is maintained by many botanic gardens retaining an association with universities and having order beds planted in such a way as to demonstrate the taxonomic relationships between different groups of plants. Usually the plants in botanic gardens are labelled to show both their scientific and common name and their countries of natural distribution. The labels also carry on accession number, so that records can be maintained of the individual plants in cultivation. It is this scientific tradition that distinguishes botanic gardens from other kinds of parks and gardens. Behind the scenes many of the world's leading botanic gardens maintain reference collections of dried plants in herbaria. These are vitally important in classifying and naming plant species and in preparing reference books such as floras, checklists and monographs. Increasingly these reference collections are computerized and available online, so that botanical information can be shared around the world.

## OPPORTUNITIES FOR RESEARCH

Research is one of the major functions of botanic gardens. Many botanic gardens provide unique opportunities to study plants of particular ecosytems, for example plants from the rainforest, prairies or desert. The Turpan Eremophytes Botanical Garden is a relatively

Seed banks are maintained by many botanic gardens as a means of preserving rare and threatened plant species for research, propagation and, where possible, return to the wild.

Photo: Board of Trustees of the Royal Botanic Gardens, Kew

"I dreamt; and in my dream
I was a butterfly.
I woke, or is it simply
That, weary of the sky,
Some butterfly is sleeping
And dreams that it is I?"

Chuang Chou

「昔者莊周夢為胡蝶。栩栩然胡蝶也。自喻適
志與。不知周也。俄然覺。則遽遽然周與。
不知周之夢為胡蝶與。胡蝶之夢為周與。
周與胡蝶。則必有分矣。此之謂物化」

莊子：齊物論

The Butterfly Garden at Kadoorie Farm and Botanic Garden in Hong Kong. Poetry and artwork are features of many botanic gardens, helping connect people with nature.

young garden established in the Gobi Desert region of Xinjiang, China, in 1976. The harsh environment of this garden – at the lowest elevation of any garden in the world and with the highest temperatures in China – provides opportunities for research into desert plants, their uses by Uygur people and the conservation of the desert flora; one particular aspect of research is desert stabilization and reafforestation. The research undertaken ranges from plant discovery, identification and cataloguing of plant uses to the establishment of new species in cultivation, and from ecological research and the impact of environmental change to a wide range of biochemical analysis.

## A GREEN OASIS IN URBAN AREAS

As well as having a scientific role, botanic gardens often also provide a haven for birds and other wildlife, and of course they provide oases of green for people living and working in urban areas. For many urban children they can provide a unique opportunity to connect with nature. The Kadoorie Farm and Botanic Garden in the New Territories of Hong Kong provides a wonderful contrast to the downtown metropolis a short distance away and provides habitat for a wide variety of mammals, birds and rare butterflies. New York Botanical Garden has a large area of native forest within its grounds and since 1987 has run the Bronx Green-Up programme, working with individuals and community groups to improve deprived urban neighbourhoods through the creation of community gardens, roof gardens, school projects, tree plantings and workshops. Kew, a short distance from one of the world's busiest airports, is a wonderful place to watch birds. The plant collections and rich invertebrate fauna support over 40 regularly breeding species of bird in the gardens. The presence of a small collection of captive birds, and the provision of birdfeeders, help to make the wild birds less wary of people than they would usually be.

Botanic gardens continue to be developed around the globe. More than half all the world's botanic gardens have been established since 1950 and at least a hundred have been developed over the past 15 years. Each botanic garden is different, its unique characteristics reflecting historical origins and current purpose, style of plantings and visitor attractions.

# Chapter 2

# SAVING PLANTS

Plants are a vital part of the world's biological diversity and an essential resource for human well-being. Yet despite their fundamental importance, thousands of species are threatened with extinction. It is currently estimated that as many as 100,000 species are at serious risk: about a quarter of all known flowering plants. The implications of their possible disappearance are huge.

The precise number of threatened plant species is not yet known. In 1997, IUCN published a global plant Red List which included over 30,000 plant species of conservation concern. This list represented many years of research by botanists to assess the rarity of species around the world. Inevitably, regions like Europe and North America were relatively well known botanically, but for other parts of the world with rich floras – such as Southeast Asia and South America – the data was harder to collect. Efforts to update the 1997 list and achieve an accurate assessment of the number of threatened plants are ongoing and speeding up.

# A GLOBAL APPROACH TO CONSERVATION

Wild plants form the basis for healthy, functioning ecosystems, helping to regulate climate, soil fertility and water supply. Many plant species are of major economic importance as the source of products such as timber, fruits, nuts, resins and gums. Worldwide, 2,000 million people depend on wood for cooking and fuel; millions of others depend on wild plants for food and medicines. The loss of species may impact directly on peoples' livelihoods, especially in poorer parts of the world.

*The loss of even one species diminishes the earth's store of biological diversity, for once eliminated, a species cannot be recovered or regenerated. All possibilities the species had for bettering life are gone, including its potential to provide the basis of life-saving medicines or new or improved foodstuffs to feed a burgeoning human population. Species losses are also felt at the genetic, community and landscape levels. When a species is gone so is its genetic heritage.*
Dallmeier, 1998

The need for conservation has been recognized, at a local level, for hundreds, if not thousands of years, but it is only over the past thirty or forty years that there has been a realization of the global scale of extinctions and the need for concerted international action. Clearly, action is needed to directly combat the threats to wild plants. Major threats include unsustainable exploitation of plant species, either for local use or international trade; the impact of introduced invasive species which can overwhelm fragile floras; habitat modification and destruction; and, increasingly, the impact of climate change. Faced with such an onslaught we need to come up with a range of solutions.

Wherever possible, the best option is to protect plant species in their natural habitats. National parks, nature reserves and other forms of protected area are vitally important in this regard and large swathes of land have already been set aside for conservation purposes, giving protection to the plants that grow there. Very often the protected areas have been selected primarily for their landscape value, or for the protection of charismatic mammals or birds. Nevertheless, the wild plants growing in these locations should benefit, particularly where the areas are well managed. Additional protected areas need to be created in areas of high plant diversity, for example in Madagascar and South Africa. Priority areas for plant conservation are generally well known, but conflicting pressures on land use can be intense.

More than 400 botanic gardens around the world manage natural areas for conservation within their boundaries, and are also involved in the study and conservation of plants outside the garden walls. The Fairchild Tropical Botanic Garden in Miami is an example of this, helping to map, monitor and research native plants and plant communities of south Florida. As part of this work, a Conservation Action Plan is

PAGE 24: *Sophora toro-miro* was described as a new species from a single surviving tree found in the vast extinct crater, Rano Kao, on Easter Island.

LEFT: The destruction of huge swathes of tropical rainforest threatens many thousands of plant species in Madagascar, an island on which 80 per cent of the wild plants grow nowhere else on earth.

produced each year, outlining recommended actions to be undertaken by land managers and researchers for the protection of 27 of the rare plant species of the area.

Ex-situ conservation, which is the preservation of plants outside their natural habitats, provides an insurance against species extinction. Ex-situ collections provide a valuable source of plant material which can be used for the reintroduction of threatened species to the wild and for the restoration of damaged or degraded habitats. Such collections also facilitate research on endangered plants, which is often necessary for the success of programmes for the recovery of threatened species. For some plants, where natural habitat is no longer available, ex-situ conservation may be the only option. Although botanic gardens play a role in both in-situ and ex-situ plant conservation, they are more usually associated with ex-situ conservation of wild plants because they are the main institutions equipped

to do this. Behind the scenes of many of the great botanic gardens of the world are laboratories, greenhouses, field nurseries and seed banks dedicated to the ex-situ survival of threatened plants.

## PIONEERING WORK

The Institute for Plant Conservation at Chicago Botanic Garden provides an example of the pioneering work being carried out by botanic gardens to ensure that plant species have a secure future. The Chicago Botanic Garden (CBG) opened in 1972 to serve as a centre for plant collections, education, and research. It describes its purpose as "to promote the enjoyment, understanding, and conservation of plants and the natural world". The garden covers over 156 hectares, of which over 80 hectares are native habitats with woodland, prairie and aquatic ecosystems. In 1997, the garden initiated a

The one-mile stretch of the Skokie River that runs through Chicago Botanic Botanic Garden is one of three natural areas in the garden. It serves as a demonstration site that offers natural methods of enhancing the local waterways.

Photo: Robin Carlson

research programme on threatened plants, which has developed into the Institute for Plant Conservation. Its four main areas of work are ex-situ conservation, restoration research, regional flora and conservation training. The garden has a state-of-the-art seed biology laboratory that serves as a regional resource for seed cleaning, storage, viability testing and determining germination protocols. Institute scientists investigate the effects of invasive species, disturbance and change of land use, as well as the impact of mankind.

In 2003, CBG joined Seeds of Success, a consortium of US conservation organizations and agencies contributing seeds to the Millennium Seed Bank at the Royal Botanic Gardens, Kew. Through this partnership, CBG is collecting and banking seeds of the entire tallgrass prairie flora, approximately 1,500 species. It also actively monitors the flora of the region around Chicago, focusing on rare and invasive plant species. In

2000, CBG initiated a local monitoring project, Plants of Concern, designed to collect population data on the region's rare plants.

Many other botanic gardens around the world are making similar efforts to conserve the natural flora. Without the efforts already made many species would have been lost and, sadly, some of the world's most threatened plants now survive only in cultivation. One famous example is the Franklin Tree, *Franklinia alatamaha*. This attractive small tree with fragrant cream flowers was discovered by plantsman John Bartram and his son William in 1765. It grew in acidic boggy soils along the banks of the Alatahama River in the American State of Georgia. The only species in its genus, *Franklinia alatamaha* was named after Dr Benjamin Franklin, one of the drafters and signatories of the American Declaration of Independence. It is thought that the Franklin Tree was naturally rare in its natural habitat and that overcollection by nurserymen contributed to its extinction. This beautiful species was last seen in the wild 200 years ago, and numerous expeditions to rediscover the plant have failed. Fortunately, it is easily raised from seed and is now a popular garden plant. Other plant species that are extinct or close to extinction in the wild but continue to thrive in botanic gardens are listed on page 150.

Ex-situ conservation is particularly important in small islands where there is high degree of endemism and land is at a premium. Many island ecosystems are highly threatened as a result of tourism development and the spread of introduced species. Introduced animals such as goats, pigs, cats and rats have historically devastated the biodiversity of oceanic islands and introduced weedy plants have had a similar effect. In the Indian Ocean, for example, the native plants of Mauritius have suffered as a result of invasive weeds such as *Ligustrum walkeri, Rubus* and *Ardisia* spp.

The long-term storage of pollen, seed or genetic material of plants provides a vital insurance mechanism for the future. Botanic gardens also have the skills to propagate and cultivate rare wild plants, so that the small population sizes of rare or threatened species can be artificially increased. New techniques of micro-propagation developed over the past forty years have greatly enhanced the potential for rescuing plant species that have been reduced to a handful of individuals in the wild. These techniques were originally developed for agricultural and horticultural crop species, but have now been used with a wide range of rare and threatened wild species, including orchids, ferns, woody plants, succulents and carnivorous plant species.

More recently, micropropagation techniques have been successfully developed for rare and threatened mosses and liverworts. The Royal Botanic Gardens, Kew has, for example, been working on the ex-situ conservation of endangered UK species of these tiny but ecologically important plants. This work, which began in 2000, initially concentrated on the development of methodologies for the collection, sterilization to remove contaminants, tissue culture and cryopreservation of the rare mosses and liverworts. Cryopreservation is the storage of living material at very low temperatures in liquid nitrogen – material preserved in this way is maintained in a state of suspended animation and therefore does not become adapted to growing in culture. The work at Kew has

The Franklin Tree is an example of a species that is no longer found in the wild but which still survives in cultivation. Approximately 10 per cent of all known tree species are threatened with extinction in the wild, with cultivation likely to play a role in saving at least some of them.

Photo: Tony Kirkham

*Cinnamomum verum* is an invasive tree that threatens the native plant species of the Seychelles.

progressed to the stage of researching the reintroduction of mosses and liverworts species to their natural environments, in close collaboration with the agencies responsible in the UK for the conservation of natural habitats and the wildlife they support.

## A GLOBAL STRATEGY

The need for botanic gardens to coordinate their work in plant conservation has been recognized since the 1970s. The Botanic Gardens Conservation Co-ordinating Body was established in 1979 as a Specialist Group of IUCN and with a small secretariat at the Royal Botanic Gardens, Kew. By 1990, an independent organization, Botanic Gardens Conservation International (BGCI), had evolved from its roots in IUCN. BGCI continues to operate as the main coordinating body for botanic gardens worldwide, with over 550 member gardens in over 110 countries. A primary concern of BGCI over the years has been to provide a means by which botanic gardens around the world can share information and news about their activities, programmes and new developments in conservation and environmental education. BGCI has also helped to develop global policies to support plant conservation, most notably the Global Strategy for Plant Conservation of the Convention on Biological Diversity (CBD).

The CBD is an international agreement to which 188 countries are signatories, and which provides a legal framework for the conservation of all biodiversity at the ecosystem, species and genetic level. This international agreement was a major result of deliberations at the United Nations Conference on Environment and Development (UNCED) the global summit held in Rio de Janeiro in 1992. Commonly known as the Rio Conference, the 1992 meeting is often used as a benchmark to measure international progress in the conservation of biodiversity. The aims of the CBD are the conservation of biological diversity, the sustainable use of its components and the fair and equitable sharing of the benefits arising from the use of genetic resources.

Even when the Convention came into force, botanists remained concerned that plants were missing out in terms of conservation action and allocation of resources. A call for action was made at the International Botanical Congress held in St Louis in 1999. After considerable

consultation and lobbying of governments, a Global Strategy for Plant Conservation (GSPC) was agreed in April 2002 by the CBD member countries. It is a bold strategy which sets out 16 ambitious targets for the conservation and sustainable use of plant biodiversity to be met by 2010 (see page 151), providing a framework for national and regional policies on plant conservation and a basis for monitoring progress. The Strategy contributes to the World Summit on Sustainable Development biodiversity target agreed in Johannesburg in 2002: "to achieve by 2010 a significant reduction in the current and continuing rate of biodiversity loss at the global, regional and national level as a contribution to poverty alleviation and to the benefit of all life on earth".

Progress on some of the targets has been remarkably good, whereas others will be more difficult to achieve. By 2010 it is expected that a full working list of the world's flora will be developed and a preliminary list of the conservation status of all plants, building on the IUCN Red List. It is likely that the GSPC target of 60 per cent of all threatened plant species being held in ex-situ collections – such as botanic gardens – will be reached. It will, however, be harder to reach the target of ten per cent of threatened plants being included in recovery and restoration programmes. It will also be difficult for many countries to ensure that targets are met relating to the sustainable production, use and trade in plants. The target of least 30 per cent of agricultural and forest lands to be managed in a manner consistent with the conservation of plant diversity will, for example, be very challenging.

Implementation of the GSPC is primarily at a national level and botanic gardens have been closely involved in helping to make the strategy a success in different countries around the world. The Seychelles, for example, was one of the first countries to develop an integrated strategy for plant conservation in line with the GSPC. With five per cent of its native plants already extinct and another ten per cent critically endangered, the Seychelles has the highest percentage of threatened flora of any country in the world. This loss and continuing threat have come after only about 250 years of permanent human habitation on the islands. The main threats to native flora have been from the spread of alien invasive species, overcollection of medicinal plants and the impact of tourism. The initiative to develop a plant

Photo: Magnus Lidén

Cyclamen are amongst the attractive garden plants that have been collected from the wild on an unsustainable basis. Major attempts are now being made to regulate the trade from Georgia and Turkey, the two main countries of export.

conservation strategy was led by the country's smallest and newest NGO, the Plant Conservation Action Group (PCA), working closely with the National Botanic Garden of the Seychelles.

The CBD has led to new thinking on the use of biodiversity by sectors such as the agricultural and pharmaceutical industries. In the past, plant resources have been seen as gifts of nature, freely available for the development of commercially valuable crops. Many of the plant resources used to fuel global trade and generate wealth since the time of the early colonial explorers have originated in tropical countries but have been developed in Europe and North America.

In an attempt to redress the balance, the CBD has introduced the concept of equitable sharing of the benefits arising from the use of genetic resources, commonly known as 'access and benefit sharing'. Botanic gardens nowadays have to be mindful of the requirements of the CBD when they collect plants from overseas and they have developed various approaches to access and benefit sharing. These generally involve exchange of information, joint planning and implementation of research projects and provision of training. There have also been efforts to repatriate plants

and herbarium specimens which have been collected in one country and held elsewhere. An example of this is provided by the work on rhododendrons by the Royal Botanic Gardens, Edinburgh. In 1996, 200 *Rhododendron* species were returned to China to form the basis of conservation collections within their country of origin. These plants had been propagated by Edinburgh from wild-collected material. More recently, Indonesian rhododendrons have been returned to the Cibodas Botanic Garden in Java.

## CITES

Another international agreement which helps to conserve wild plants is the Convention on International Trade in Endangered Species of Wild Fauna and Flora (CITES). This is arguably the most powerful of the international biodiversity conservation agreements because its requirements are translated into national laws in all the countries that sign up to it. The Convention has been in force for over 25 years and has been ratified by over 160 countries. Botanic gardens have played an important role in the implementation of CITES for plant species and in raising awareness of the aims and requirements of the

Convention, providing much of the expertise and information needed to ensure its effective operation.

All orchids and cacti are covered by CITES, together with some other succulents, palms, bulbs such as snowdrops, *Cyclamen* and cycads. These are the groups that have been threatened by commercial collecting from the wild for gardens and greenhouses. Over the past 25 years there has been an improvement in the understanding of the threats to biodiversity and the need to link conservation with development issues. These changes are reflected in the evolution of CITES which increasingly recognizes that rural people may be dependent on the income they earn from the commercial collecting of wild species.

More attention is now directed towards the major commercial groups of internationally traded species such as timbers. This will provide a significant new challenge for CITES, which has traditionally focused more on ornamental plants, such as orchids and succulents, often the target of unscrupulous collectors. Conservation problems clearly remain for these horticultural groups and CITES implementation needs to be improved to concentrate on tackling illegal trade in endangered species such as Vietnamese Slipper

Orchids, *Paphiopedilum* spp. At the same time, with over a thousand timber species threatened by international trade, and growing awareness of the illegality associated with the timber trade, CITES clearly needs to be more involved in monitoring and controlling trade in threatened timber species.

It is important for CITES to demonstrate how it proposes to tackle the interlinked problems of biodiversity loss and poverty. As a first step, CITES is looking at the economic incentives for sustainable wildlife trade and the development of national policies to promote this. There are clear linkages between this work and the work of the Convention on Biological Diversity (CBD), which is also looking at economic incentives for biodiversity conservation and sustainable use.

Links between the work of CITES and CBD are growing generally and in the case of plants have been brought together through the GSPC. Target 11 of the Strategy calls for "No species of wild flora endangered by international trade". Reaching this ambitious target by 2010 will require increased and coordinated support from governments, NGOs and botanic gardens around the world.

# CONSERVATION AND RESTORATION

BGCI has helped botanic gardens to develop their own policies and programmes for plant conservation. At an international level the International Agenda for Botanic Gardens in Conservation sets out a comprehensive menu of options for conservation and sustainable development. Agreed in 2000, over 400 botanic gardens have signed up to the International Agenda. BGCI also maintains a global database of plant species cultivated by botanic gardens. The PlantSearch database currently records more than 100,000 species in cultivation, about 25 per cent of the total known flora. One of the main benefits of this database is that botanic gardens can compare the plants in their collections with the IUCN Red List and other lists of threatened plants. In this way they can establish the

importance of their plants for conservation purposes and prioritize the care given to rare species. The database is also used to monitor global progress towards the GSPC target on ex-situ plant conservation. BGCI is actively involved in training botanic gardens in conservation techniques to enhance the value of their conservation work, and in supporting the networking of gardens, for example in Africa, Asia, Russia and Latin America.

Botanic gardens also work together at regional and national levels to implement the conservation of plant species. In the USA, for example, the Center for Plant Conservation (CPC) is a powerful force for the conservation of US native plants, working to conserve and restore the rare native plants of the United States. About 25 per cent of native US plant species are of conservation concern and 80 per cent of these plants are related to species of agronomic importance. Based at Missouri Botanic Garden, the CPC maintains the National Collection of Endangered Plants, which contains plant material for more than 600 of the country's most threatened native plants. CPC consists of a network of 33 participating institutions located throughout the country, from Hawaii to Massachusetts. Chicago Botanic Garden and the Morton Arboretum, for example, have jointly formed the Chicago Center for Endangered Plants and work on the ex-situ conservation of 11 globally rare taxa for the CPC. CPC institutions work with threatened plants both in ex-situ collections and in the wild. Their scientists work on growing the threatened plants from seed or from cuttings, proving plant material for restoration efforts, and also assist in monitoring populations in the wild, managing habitat and restoring plants to native habitats.

The Peacock Larkspur, *Delphinium pavonaceum*, is an example of a US species that is being cared for by the CPC. This attractive white-flowered plant is found only in the Willamette Valley of Oregon. Nearly all the valley's grassland habitat has been converted to agricultural and residential use, so that the Peacock Larkspur is now restricted to fencerows and ditches where small patches of habitat have escaped destruction. The Berry Botanic Garden, located in Portland, Oregon is the National Collection garden for the Peacock Larkspur. Seeds from five sites are stored by the garden, which is particularly concerned with the conservation of endangered plants of the Pacific Northwest.

Another plant being saved by CPC is the Ventura Marsh Milkvetch, *Astragalus pycnostachyus* var. *lanosissimus*. This species was presumed extinct until it was rediscovered in sandy soil covering an oil dump in Oxnard, California. Scientists carefully collected seeds from the plant for storage by Rancho Santa Ana Botanic Garden and Santa Barbara Botanic Garden. In 2003 more than 300 milkvetch plants were planted back into the wild.

An important activity being undertaken by CPC institutions is studying the status of all plants listed under the US Endangered Species Act, looking at their potential for recovery. They work in close collaboration with major landowners and managers, including the National Park Service, to ensure an integrated approach to plant conservation. The conservation work of CPC is a model for plant conservation efforts around the world.

Techniques for the restoration of threatened plants have also been pioneered by botanic gardens in Australia. There have been noteworthy successes with some of the rare and endangered orchids of the country. In total about 120 Australian orchids are threatened with extinction. One species which has been successfully reintroduced into the wild is *Diuris purdiei*. This attractive species with brown and yellow-coloured flowers was probably once common in the coastal plain south of Perth, Western Australia; sadly, clearance for agriculture and urbanization reduced the known population of the species to fewer than 500 individuals. Joint research on the species, undertaken by the Kings Park and Botanic Gardens and the Western Australian Department of Conservation and Land Management, resulted in a comprehensive conservation recovery plan for the species. Seedlings were produced using mycorrhizal fungi to enhance germination and plantlets were also produced using tissue culture techniques. Plants from seed were also reintroduced to the wild at secure sites. A related species, *Diuris micranthera*, which is equally restricted to a small natural area near Perth, has also been successfully propagated for reintroduction to the wild.

Another species successfully reintroduced into the wild in Western Australia is the critically endangered Corrigin Grevillea, *Grevillea scapigera*, thought to be extinct in its natural habitat by 1986. Fortunately the last survivors of the species were established in tissue culture at Kings Park and Botanic Gardens and at the Royal Botanic Gardens, Sydney and, following successful micropropagation, hundreds of plants have been planted back in the wild.

Using modern techniques, it is technically possible to prevent the extinction of all plant species. Ultimately, however, plant conservation will succeed only if people value the diversity of plant species and appreciate what is being lost. The value of plant diversity is perhaps most easily understood by the millions of rural poor people who depend on plants for their food, medicines and livelihoods but may not have the means to use plants sustainably. It is too easy to overlook the importance of plants in supporting all life on earth, but botanic gardens around the world can help to remind people of this message. With an estimated 200 million visitors each year, botanic gardens have a great opportunity to inform as well as inspire.

Temperate lady slipper
orchids (*Cypripedium*
spp.) are threatened with
extinction in the wild in
both Europe and North
America. This is partly as
a result of overcollecting
in the past.

Photo: Bob Meyer

# Chapter 3

## EUROPE AND RUSSIA

Europe has a rich heritage of botanic gardens, with a history
spanning over four centuries. These gardens have influenced
the course of global development through their study and
distribution of agricultural crops and pharmaceutical ingredients.
At the same time they have always been, and continue to be,
gardens for pleasure and inspiration.

There are over 500 botanic gardens in Western Europe, most of these being in France, Germany, Italy and the United Kingdom. Botanic gardens are also well established in Eastern and Central Europe, with Poland and the Czech Republic, for example, each having 25. Russia and the former states of the USSR have about 170. Following several centuries of development concerned with crops, medicine and exotic collections, the emphasis in European botanic gardens has now shifted squarely to plant conservation, and many are now playing an active role in plans to safeguard the flora of both Europe and further afield.

# THE UNITED KINGDOM

Among the world-renowned European gardens are the Royal Botanic Gardens at Edinburgh and Kew. The Royal Botanic Garden, Edinburgh (RBGE) dates back to 1670, when two distinguished Edinburgh doctors, Andrew Balfour and Robert Sibbald, leased a small enclosure in St Anne's Yards near Holyrood Abbey. Both men had travelled widely in Europe and were familiar with the botanic garden at Leiden, which was an important centre of medical training. At this time, physicians were trained in both medicine and botany, because most drugs were derived from plants (the two disciplines did not separate into different subjects for study until the late 19th century). Balfour and Sibbald established a collection of about 900 plant taxa from their own private gardens, by collecting wild material in Scotland, and from another private collector, Patrick Murray. The purpose of the garden was to teach botany to students, to train apothecaries and to produce a Scottish Pharmacopeia.

The botanic garden moved site several times during its history and was established at its present site in Inverleith in 1820–23. Today the site, known locally as "the Botanics", is a major attraction for tourists and Scots alike, with a splendid Rock Garden and a range of glasshouses including Tropical and Temperate Palm Houses. A new project to build Scotland's first National Biodiversity Centre, near the West Gate, is due for completion in 2009.

The botanic garden has a long history of working in what are now known as biodiversity hotspots. Nepal is one example and Bhutan is another – after years of research producing a *Flora of Bhutan*, RBGE is now helping to establish a new botanic garden in Serbithang, near the Bhutanese capital. Through training and exchange programmes between Bhutan and Edinburgh, staff at the new garden are taught how to identify and propagate indigenous plants.

Many of RBGE's conservation programmes focus on oceanic islands, such as New Caledonia and Socotra, or on remote wilderness areas such as southern and central Chile. The garden also has well-established links with China and is twinned with the Kunming Institute of Botany in Yunnan. A five-year programme aims to survey the plant and animal biodiversity in one of the remotest parts of China – a mountain range straddling the border of Yunnan province and Myanmar.

The 30-hectare Inverleith site in Edinburgh offers a range of habitats for plants but, over the years, the need to find space for the growing collections of woody plants has led to the setting up of three specialist gardens at other sites in Scotland. Younger Botanic Garden (purchased in 1929) at Benmore, a splendid 50-hectare mountainside garden with a warm, wet climate, shelters some of the tallest trees in Britain, while subtropical Logan (purchased in 1969), in the far southwest, benefits from a mild climate and supports a variety of plants from warm, temperate regions. A specimen of Wollemi Pine, *Wollemia nobilis*, thought to

be extinct until several trees were discovered in Australia in the 1990s, was planted at Logan in 2006. It is a new introduction to Scotland and the first one to be planted outdoors there. The newest garden acquisition for Edinburgh is Dawyck in the Scottish Borders (purchased in 1978), a delightful woodland garden with cooler growing conditions in which rhododendrons thrive. With the Edinburgh site, the four gardens are known collectively as the National Botanic Gardens of Scotland.

Visitors to Kew never fail to be impressed by the magnificent Palm House. Designed by the architect Decimus Burton, working with the Dublin-based engineer Richard Turner, the Palm House took four years to build and was completed in 1848, seven years after the gardens were first opened to the public. Despite its

grandeur, the Kew Palm House is only about half the size of the Temperate House, which shelters a wide range of plant species native to southern Africa, Asia, Chile, the Mediterranean and New Zealand. Also designed by Decimus Burton, Kew's Temperate House took 39 years to build and was opened to the public in 1899.

Another famous Kew landmark is the Pagoda. Visitors can climb up the 253 steps and enjoy fabulous views of the gardens, London landmarks and beyond. This was built in 1761–62 as part of the development of the private botanic garden belonging to Princess Augusta, mother of King George III. The 3.6-hectare garden she created formed the nucleus for the development of the current Gardens. In 2006 another fine glasshouse was inaugurated in the form of the Alpine House. Featuring state-of-the-art air-cooling

PAGE 38: The National Botanic Garden of Wales has the largest single-span glasshouse in the world. It shelters collections of Mediterranean plants.

ABOVE: First opened in 1836, Sheffield Botanical Gardens is currently undergoing restoration to its former glory. Originally designed by Robert Marnock, the garden contains impressive Glass Pavilions which are now protected as historic buildings.

facilities, its sleek, arched form takes Kew's architecture into the 21st century, along with the elegant new bridge over the lake, designed by the minimalist architect, John Pawson. The Alpine House has cold rather than warm air pumped around the plants, simulating the mountain breezes of alpine habitats. The shape of the glasshouse produces a chimney effect, drawing warm air up and outwards, and has been designed to ensure that the miniature campanulas, helichrysum, primulas and saxifrages have the dry and bright conditions that they need to thrive.

Kew's international reputation was established by Sir Joseph Banks, a plant collector famed for his botanical heritage and his voyages with Captain Cook and Charles Darwin. Joseph Banks served as horticultural adviser at Kew from 1772 until his death in 1820. Banks was a strong supporter of Charles Darwin's theory of natural selection and encouraged Darwin's botanical research interests, including the mechanics of orchid pollination and mechanisms employed by climbing plants. A legacy of the friendship between Banks and Darwin is the *Index Kewensis*, a list of all flowering plant names from the time of Linnaeus, which is still compiled today. Darwin bequeathed money to Kew for the development of this universal plant list.

Kew is also home to one of the world's most ambitious plant conservation programmes – the Millennium Seed Bank, based at Kew's country site, Wakehurst Place in Sussex. Inaugurated in 2000, the Wellcome Trust Millennium Building now contains collections representing around 97 per cent of the UK's native flowering plants, conifers and ferns. The Millennium Seed Bank is also helping to coordinate a network of European seed banks, which seeks to share expertise and facilities, thereby avoiding duplication of effort across continental Europe. Further afield, the Millennium Seed Bank aims to collect and conserve ten per cent of the world's flowering plants and conifers (some 24,000 species), mainly from the arid areas of the world, by 2010. Drylands cover a third of the earth's land surface, including many of the world's poorest countries, and support almost one-fifth of its population. The most immediate threat to dryland areas and the plant species that can survive the harsh conditions is desertification due to overgrazing and agriculture. The seeds stored by Kew will help to ensure the potential restoration of

Photo: Board of Trustees of the Royal Botanic Gardens, Kew

dryland areas in the future. Around the world, such activities are undertaken collaboratively, ensuring that research, training and capacity-building relationships are developed with the countries where the seeds are collected, collaborations based on principles of the CBD, respecting national sovereignty and supporting national biodiversity conservation strategies. Benefit-sharing, in the form of duplicate seed storage, data exchange, technology transfer and training are all essential components of the work of the Millennium Seed Bank.

The Seed Bank is just one of numerous conservation projects undertaken by Kew. Important research into Bryophytes (mosses, liverworts and hornworts) aims to establish a comprehensive collection for conservation needs, so that material can be propagated and used for reintroduction into natural habitats. Despite their small size, Bryophytes play an important role in ecosystems, acting as a buffer system for other plants. Bog mosses (*Sphagnum* spp.), which form peat bogs, are a well-known example, good at taking in and retaining carbon dioxide.

At Kew's Jodrell Laboratory, research is being undertaken to find natural remedies for the treatment of diabetes, a condition that affects over two million people in the UK alone. So far, over 500 species of plant with antidiabetic activity have been identified, each containing a group of compounds known as sugar-mimics. Kew also incorporates the only Traditional Chinese Medicine Authentication Centre in the UK. The Centre's work involves identifying plants that are brought into the UK for use in traditional Chinese medicine, in order to check their authenticity and protect the safe use of the herbs and promote patient safety.

Kew is also involved in many projects around the world, including training programmes on plant identification and collection techniques in countries such as Thailand and Malaysia. These are targeted at horticulture workers and forest rangers, as well as officials such as customs officers expected to implement CITES.

The small island of Monserrat in the West Indies experienced a colossal volcanic eruption in 1996 and much of the southern side of the island is still smothered in ash. Along with other partners, Kew has been involved in a plan to help the local people conserve the central hills and establish the island's first national park. Inventory work has already led to the rediscovery of several threatened species. A population of the endemic shrub *Rondeletia buxifolia*, not seen since 1979, was located in the north of the island in November 2005. The plant will be protected locally and at Kew by ex-situ conservation. Plants conserved in this way eventually join the living collections at Kew and go on public display.

Photo: Royal Horticultural Society

The RHS Garden at Wisley is a showcase for the Royal Horticultural Society, organizer of the world-renowned Chelsea Flower Show.

In 2003, the Royal Botanic Gardens, Kew was awarded UNESCO World Heritage Site status in recognition of its fine landscape gardens and leading contribution to the study of plant diversity and economic botany around the world. Kew's World Heritage status acknowledges that "the landscape features and architectural features of the gardens reflect considerable artistic influences both with regard to the European continent and to more distant regions. The landscape gardens and the edifices created by celebrated artists such as Charles Bridgeman, William Kent, Lancelot 'Capability' Brown and William Chambers reflect the beginning of movements which were to have international influence".

The Royal Horticultural Society (RHS) celebrated its bicentenary in 2004. The RHS now maintains four gardens in the UK: at Wisley in Surrey, Harlow Carr in Yorkshire, Rosemoor in Devon and Hyde Hall in Essex. The garden at Wisley was given to the Society in 1903 by Sir Thomas Hanbury, a wealthy Quaker who had established the famous garden of La Mortola, on the Italian Riviera. The garden at Wisley was originally created by George Ferguson Wilson, a man of many talents who was successful in business, as well as being an inventor, a keen gardener and a former Treasurer of the Society. His garden developed fine collections of lilies, gentians, Japanese irises, primulas and water plants. When Wisley was handed over to the RHS, it enabled the Society to expand its trials of flowers, vegetables and fruit – work that had been undertaken since 1860 at a site in Chiswick. The

trials remain an important component of the work at Wisley.

The RHS trains gardeners at all levels and encourages sustainable horticulture. It helps teachers with resources and advice, and offers expert advice to gardeners. As part of its mission to promote excellence in horticulture in public spaces, the RHS also organizes the annual 'Britain in Bloom' campaign to stimulate interest in public planting and improvements in the environment at local level (biodiversity was the theme for 2006). The RHS holds world-famous flower shows each year, the best known being the Chelsea Flower Show, held each May in the grounds of the Royal Hospital in Chelsea.

The Chelsea area of London is also home to England's second oldest garden, the Chelsea Physic Garden, founded in 1673 by the Worshipful Society of Apothecaries. Originally intended as a garden for the study of medicinal plants, and chosen for its proximity to

Sir Hans Sloane, a famous early botanist associated with the introduction to Britain of chocolate, is commemorated by a statue in the Chelsea Physic Garden. He owned the land on which the garden was established.

Photo: Board of Trustees of the Chelsea Physic Garden

the River Thames, which gave it a milder climate, by the 1700s the Physic Garden had initiated an international seed exchange programme, which is still in operation today. It retains an important role in the 21st century, safeguarding and researching the properties, origins and conservation of over 5,000 species. Among its collections are rare and endangered plants from the islands of Crete, Madeira and the Canary Islands. The collection of endemic Cretan plants is grown on the restored Pond Rockery, originally built in 1773 with pieces from the Tower of London and Iceland lava donated by Sir Joseph Banks.

In a completely different style, one of Britain's newest sites devoted to the celebration of plant diversity is the Eden Project, a series of vast biomes constructed in an abandoned china clay quarry in Cornwall. One of the landmark Millennium projects built in the UK to celebrate the year 2000, Eden's mission is to promote care for the environment through displays of plantings from the humid tropics and warm temperate regions of the world. The Eden landscape has transformed a previously derelict site, intermingling stunning works of art with the unusual plants. The project has proved very effective in reinterpreting the botanic garden message and attracting

a new audience. Behind the scenes, Eden supports initiatives such as Edinburgh's Conifer Conservation Programme, the preservation of the Seychellois Coco-de-mer, and a training programme for researchers working on mangroves. Eden also sponsors graduate research at Cornwall's Falmouth College of Art, which will look at uses for plant-based materials and structures.

Another Millennium project, the National Botanic Garden of Wales, occupies a lovely open site in west Wales. In collaboration with the National Museum of Wales and the Countryside Council for Wales, the botanic garden is working to safeguard the survival of rare Welsh plants such as *Sorbus leyana* and a hawkweed found only at a single site in the Brecon Beacons. Plants that are declining in number are also given protection here, including the Greater Butterfly Orchid and Whorled Caraway. The Great Glasshouse, designed by Norman Foster, reproduces a Mediterranean environment and offers a refuge for rare plants such as the Western Australian shrub *Grevillea maccutcheonii*, which was micropropagated at the King's Park Botanic Garden in Perth, and flowered for the first time in the Great Glasshouse in 2003.

This 18th-century print after Canaletto shows a view of the Chelsea Physic Garden from the south bank of the Thames. The Royal Hospital is on the far right.

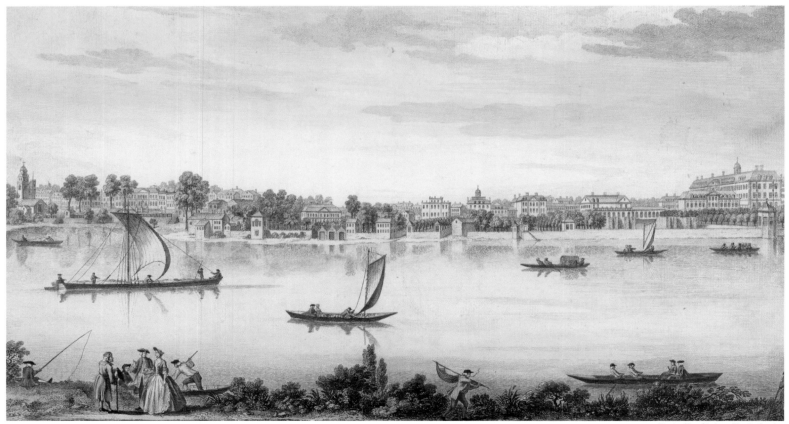

Photo: The Chelsea Physic Garden

# IRELAND

The National Botanic Garden, Dublin, is Ireland's premier botanic garden with a huge collection of around 20,000 species and cultivars. The gardens cover approximately 19.5 hectares, taking in the natural flood plain of the River Tolka. They include a spectacular range of four glasshouses dominated by another of the Victorian Richard Turner's architectural masterpieces, the so-called Curvilinear Range. Construction on this began in 1843 and the first phase was complete by the time Queen Victoria visited Dublin in 1849. The glasshouses were restored and re-opened to the public for the bicentenary of the gardens in 1995. One wing of the Curvilinear Range displays plants from South Africa, warm temperate parts of Western Australia, and South America. The other wing contains a collection of Southeast Asian rhododendrons given to the garden by the Royal Botanic Garden, Edinburgh, and the central part of the house contains a collection of gymnosperms.

The gardens were established in the Glasnevin area of Dublin by the Dublin Society for Promoting Husbandry and Other Useful Arts, with the intention of promoting the scientific study of agriculture. Initially the gardens displayed comparative plantings of different crops and demonstrations of the latest agricultural machinery, serving more as a model farm than a botanic garden. By the 1830s the study of botany had overtaken that of agriculture and by 1838 the basic shape of the gardens had been established, largely due to the curator Ninian Niven. Plants from around the world were introduced to the gardens and close contact was maintained with the botanical gardens of Kew and Edinburgh.

Nowadays, notable features of the National Botanic Garden include the rockery, herbaceous borders, the rose garden, alpine yard, vegetable garden, arboretum, extensive shrub collections and wall plants. An alley of yew trees known as Addison's Walk is thought to date back to before 1740. The Irish National Herbarium, with a million dried plant specimens, and the comprehensive botanical library are also located in Glasnevin.

Herbaceous borders at the National Botanic Garden in Dublin add colour to this very attractive and scientifically important centre for botanical and horticultural study.

Photo: Peter Wyse Jackson

# GERMANY

ermany's 100 botanical gardens, many with a long history going back as far as the Renaissance, attract over 14 million visitors each year. The Botanischer Garten der Universität Bonn occupies a particularly appealing site in the grounds of a medieval castle, partially surrounded by a moat. In 1650 a Renaissance garden stood here, which was followed by a Baroque garden in the 1720s, and the site became a scientific institution in 1818, when the university was founded. The mild climate makes it possible to grow a range of temperate plants out in the open. There are order beds, an arboretum, a geographical section with plants grouped by place of origin, a biotope containing indigenous species, with special emphasis on endangered species from the area around Bonn, and an educational garden that demonstrates ecological relationships.

The glasshouses are divided into major climatic zones, including the Palm House, Mangrove House, the Victoria House with its famous Giant Water-lilies, the Succulent House with Welwitschias from Namibia, and two Orchid Houses. The botanic garden provides living collections for the work of the scientists at the Botanical Institute, which includes research into biodiversity loss (the Institute is closely associated with study of the flora of the Cape Verde islands), habitat protection, the evolutionary history of flowering plants, and mapping and analysis of geographical patterns. Another area of

The succulent collection at Bonn Botanic Garden.

Photo: BGCI

research concerns the adaptation of natural plant properties for use in technology and new products. The self-cleaning characteristics of Sacred Lotus leaves, for example, have been applied with great success to paint finishes and roof tiles.

Berlin's botanic garden has a history of around 300 years. It has relocated several times in the past and now occupies a spacious site at Dahlem in the south of the city. 22,000 different plant species are dispersed over 43 hectares, including an arboretum with around 1,800 species of trees and shrubs. Nearly a third of the garden is taken up by a collection of plants arranged geographically, one of the biggest of its kind, where visitors can walk around northern hemisphere habitats from the Alps to the Himalayas and on through to Japan and North America. Twelve rock gardens feature plants from mountains, forests, dunes and steppes, and were designed by Adolf

Engler, the first director when the garden moved to Dahlem about 100 years ago. An aquatic and marsh plant garden is increasingly important as marshy habitats dry out and their plants are put at risk. Many of the species grown in the garden have been lost from their natural habitats. Very popular is the display of about 230 medicinal plants, arranged in the shape of a human body, with information on their pharmacological importance.

There are also extensive glasshouses. The main tropical greenhouse (closed for renovation at the time of writing) is one of the largest in the world, and the site is also home to a public botanical museum, a large botanical library and a herbarium with 3.5 million specimens. Behind the scenes, the botanical staff carry out a very full research programme, including several collaborative projects with countries such as Greece, Cuba, El Salvador and Yemen.

The Mediterranean House of Berlin's botanic garden has important displays of Mediterranean evergreen forest and shrubby 'garigue' vegetation. It also shelters a special collection of plants from the Canary Islands, Madeira and the Azores.

Photo: Botanischer Garten Berlin-Dahlem/I. Haas

# RUSSIA

The Botanical Gardens of the M.V. Lomonosov Moscow State University (MSU) were founded in 1706 and form one of the oldest botanical institutions in Russia. Tropical and subtropical plants can be seen at the hothouses at the garden's original site, located where the "chemists' garden" was established 300 years ago by Peter the Great. Moscow University acquired ownership of the garden in 1805. With the building of the new premises for Moscow State University and the laying out of a new garden, the former Botanical Gardens, a historical and cultural monument of Moscow, became its branch. During construction of MSU's new premises at the Lenin (now Vorobyovy) Hills, a new university garden was laid out. More than 6,000 plant species, varieties and cultivars were planted in an area of 40 hectares. The garden includes an arboretum, an area devoted to montane plants, taxonomic collections and plots demonstrating useful and ornamental plants.

The Main Botanical Gardens of Moscow (MBG) form one of the biggest botanic gardens in Europe. They are situated in the northern part of Moscow, covering an area of 331 hectares. More than half of this territory is occupied by well-preserved woodland, which includes a reserve of ancient oaks and meadow vegetation. The cultivated section of the gardens includes a cascade of ponds, decorative entrances, the Garden of Permanent Blooming, a heather garden and the only Japanese garden in Russia. The gardens also contain a large research complex: the MBG is a scientific-research institute of the Department of Biological Sciences, part of the Russian Academy of Sciences. The main objective of research here is the creation of a comprehensive theoretical basis for plant introduction and acclimatization, with a view to the most effective application of world plant resources. Biodiversity conservation is also a key research activity. Living collections include more than 21,000 taxa of wild and cultivated plants with an emphasis on economic species. The gardens have around 8,000 different taxa of ornamental plants and more than 500 species of plants used in medicine.

The Botanic Garden of Irkutsk State University is the only botanic garden in the Lake Baikal region. Its mission is "to protect and enrich the flora of the Lake Baikal area and the world for people through public education, collection, propagation, research, and conservation of plants". The garden is principally an educational tool and maintains a herbarium, seed bank and three living collections.

Photo: A. Barinov

# GEORGIA

Situated between two mountain ridges in the deep canyon of the river Tsavkisistskali, the Tbilisi Botanic Garden in Georgia was founded in 1636. The garden overlooks the oldest parts of the city, and since 1916 its objective has been the conservation and propagation of the rich flora of the Caucasus region. Currently over a hundred vulnerable species are grown by the garden, including globally threatened Caucasian endemics such as wild snowdrops (*Galanthus* spp.) and trees such as the oak *Quercus pontica*, a species with a limited natural range in Georgia and Turkey. In addition to the conservation collections, natural vegetation within the garden has been protected since 1901, particularly within the upper parts of the garden and along the river banks.

Photo: M. Smith/Board of Trustees of the Royal Botanic Gardens, Kew

OPPOSITE: Moscow's Main Botanical Gardens have formal plantings as well as a nature reserve within the extensive grounds.

LEFT: Tbilisi's stunning botanic garden is now important as a centre for the conservation of threatened snowdrop species and other attractive plants.

# FRANCE

Established in 1626 by King Louis XIII's doctors, Jean Hérouard and Guy de la Brosse, the Jardin des Plantes in Paris began life as a medicinal herb garden. It was opened to the public in 1640 and is now one of the great parks of Paris, covering a total of 28 hectares. As well as a fine alpine house containing over 3,000 different species, France's Natural History Museum stands in the grounds, as does a School of Botany that trains botanists and runs an international seed exchange programme. Three hectares are devoted to horticultural displays, including a rose garden. The garden expanded rapidly during the reign of Louis XIV, when hothouses were built to accommodate plants from France's colonial possessions.

The Jardin Botanique de Lyon (Parc de la Tête d'Or) occupies a broad site at a bend in the River Rhône and provides a welcome oasis of green in the city. The 600 or more trees in the arboretum include an example of *Pinus bungeana* (Laceback Pine), which probably derives from the first batch of seeds sent from China to Kew Gardens in 1860. Many of the plants in the gardens have recently been relabelled with the IUCN categories indicating their degree of risk – endangered, threatened, vulnerable, and so on.

The network of Conservatoires Botaniques Nationaux in France together form the main agency responsible for safeguarding the native flora. The Conservatoire Botanique National de Brest, at the extreme west of Brittany, was established in 1975 with the specific aim of protecting the flora of the Massif Armoricain and neighbouring islands. Today the institute cares for rare and endangered plants from Brittany and Basse-Normandie, parts of the Pays-de-la-Loire and Poitou-Charentes, representing 14 per cent of France's total land surface.

At the far southeast of the country, the Conservatoire Botanique National Méditerranéen de Porquerolles offers one of France's loveliest settings for conservation – a beautiful wooded island off the coast of Provence. Around 85 per cent of France's vascular flora is represented across the south of France, and levels of endemism are high. Porquerolles, 4.3 miles long and 1.8

Photo: Frédéric Muller

Photo: Service Audiovisuel/MNHN

miles wide, is the largest of the three islands in the Gulf of Hyères. It has been protected from uncontrolled tourist development since 1971, when the French government bought four-fifths of the island. The island itself supports over 700 different species of plant, including rare species such as *Genista linifolia* and the endemic *Delphinium requienii*. Threatened Corsican endemics such as *Naufraga balearica*, *Anchusa crispa* and *Silene velutina* have all been successfully propagated on Porquerolles, which specializes in the protection of rare and threatened Mediterranean plants.

The Conservatoire also collects traditional varieties of fruiting trees, to prevent old varieties disappearing from the genetic bank. It is a valuable reserve for the future, with over 110 varieties of olive tree, 150 peach trees and more than 20 varieties of almond. A seed bank is also maintained at the site.

# MONACO

A very different kind of garden can be seen at the Jardin Exotique in Monaco, which gives a dramatically steep rocky home to a vibrant collection of cacti and succulents. Over 7,000 species are represented here, including the rare *Aloe eminens*, a 150-year-old example of *Echinocactus grusonii* and a splendid example of *Neobuxbaumia polylopha*, over six metres tall. The Exotic Garden also houses a Botanical Centre, where specialists work on conservation projects such as the cultivation and propagation of threatened cacti and succulents. A seed list is published annually and sent to over 50 countries.

Photo: Jardin Exotique de Monaco

Photo: Jardin Exotique de Monaco

# ITALY

Italy, with a long tradition of botanic gardens going back to the Renaissance period, currently has over 100 botanic gardens. One of the earliest, the botanic garden of Florence, dates from the time of Cosimo de' Medici. Founded in 1545 as a Giardino dei Semplici, or garden of simples (as medicinal herbs were known), the garden was the third to be established after Padua and Pisa. It covers a little more than two hectares, retaining much of its original layout, with hot and temperate houses for tropical plants, medicinal plants, and some fine old examples of sequoias and cedars.

Elsewhere in Italy there are small but thriving university botanic gardens in Turin, Bologna and Rome, as well as in the Sicilian towns of Catania and Palermo. These last two gardens have fine displays of cacti and succulents and both operate seed and gene banks for the conservation of local flora.

An Italian garden that has attracted a lot of attention since its extensive renovation in the 1980s is the lovely coastal garden at La Mortola, the Villa Hanbury, at the western end of the Italian Riviera, close to the border with France. The property was bought in 1867 by Sir Thomas Hanbury, a businessman and keen plantsman. The south-facing headland, protected by the mountains behind it, benefits from a particularly mild, equable climate, and Sir Thomas wanted to establish a garden of acclimatization on the site. Following restoration, the Villa Hanbury is once again home to a wide variety of Mediterranean and exotic plants, with a range of olive and pine trees, and shrubs including Myrtle, Laurel, Rosemary and Broom. The south-facing part is planted with agaves, aloes, opuntias, cacti and yuccas, giving the garden a very exotic look.

The garden, at its height under the Hanburys, was perhaps more famous in Great Britain than in Italy. Before the Second World War, *The Times* used to publish a list of the plants flowering at Villa Hanbury on New Year's Day, to emphasize to the garden-loving British how mild the climate was throughout the year in the Mediterranean. Today, the garden belongs to the Botanical Institute of the University of Genoa.

The stunning setting of La Mortola Botanic Garden, on the Italian Riviera near Ventimiglia.

A native plant of Asia, *Chionanthus retusus* is cultivated in botanic gardens around the world. This particular specimen is in the Orto Botanico in Padua, Italy.

Photo: Charlie Jarvis

# SPAIN

Within Europe, the natural diversity of plant species increases as you travel from north to south. The Mediterranean region is extremely diverse in terms of wild plants and, with its abundance of local endemics, is considered to be one of the world's biodiversity hotspots. After several thousand years of intensive agriculture, and with the recent pressures of urban development and tourism, many species are now under threat. Wild anemones, daffodils, orchids and peonies are some of the many attractive plants that may be lost. Botanic gardens in the region are playing a major role in plant conservation and some have been created specifically for this purpose. The Soller Botanic Garden on the island of Majorca was, for example, established in the 1980s as a centre of conservation, for the study and understanding of the Mediterranean flora. The Balearic Islands, of which Majorca is the largest, have over 150 endemic plants. The Soller Botanic Garden has 130 of these species in cultivation and carries out research into their reproductive biology.

In southern Spain, the botanic garden of Cordoba is also dedicated to plant conservation, with a focus on the rich and threatened flora of Andalusia. This province of Spain has a vascular flora with around 4,000 taxa at the species and subspecies level. Of these, 1,074 are either endemics or have a narrow distribution. Nearly 70 taxa are considered to be extinct or endangered, and half of these occur only in Andalusia. In total, more than 1,000 plant taxa need to be protected, either because they are severely threatened or because they are extremely rare. Approximately 17 per cent of the Andalusian territory is set aside for conservation, but many of the threatened plants are located outside the Natural Parks or Reserves. The Cordoba Botanic Garden was established in 1981 by a group of researchers working on germplasm banks and

Photo: BGCI

ABOVE: Cycads in
Barcelona Botanic Garden.

OPPOSITE: *Dracaena
draco,* a 'Vulnerable'
species endemic to the
Canary Islands, here
growing in the Viera y
Clavijo Botanic Garden.

conservation plan for the species is being developed by Cordoba Botanic Garden.

Andalusia has a great ethnobotanical heritage; some of its regions are rich both in traditional knowledge and in plants that are important for their medicinal or food properties, or for their use in crafts and folklore. Species of medicinal value include Andalusian endemics such as *Sideritis glacialis, Pterocephalus spathulatus, Digitalis nevadensis* and *Artemisia granatensis.* Some crops have wild relatives in the region, requiring special consideration in the management and conservation programmes (for example, certain species of the genera *Cynara, Allium* and *Beta).*

## THE CANARY ISLANDS

The Viera y Clavijo Botanic Garden in Gran Canaria is one of the world's leading botanic gardens dedicated to plant conservation, with both living collections and a seed bank. The seed bank, established in 1983, now maintains seed from all the endemic plants of the Canary Islands as well as duplicate samples of seed from other parts of Spain. The Canary Islands, one of the world's biodiversity hotspots, are home to around 1,200 native plant species, of which 500 are endemic and more than 200 are threatened with extinction at a global scale. Natural habitats that are under threat on the islands include the laurel forests, which are of great ecological importance both in controlling erosion and in influencing local rainfall. These forests are believed to be relicts of a flora which covered much of southern Europe and north Africa during the Tertiary period. They contain a high number of rare and endemic species, such as *Arbutus canariensis,* locally known as Madroño. On Tenerife, the laurel forests have been reduced by more than 90 per cent, chiefly as a result of clearance for agriculture.

Madroño, one of the threatened tree species in cultivation at the Viera y Clavijo Botanic Garden, is a cloudforest tree known only from around ten populations in the wild, probably containing no more than 10,000 individuals. Madroño is an attractive small tree well suited to cultivation in warm temperate climates. It has white or greenish bell-shaped flowers, often tinged with pink, and edible fruit similar to that of the strawberry tree, *Arbutus unedo.* The fruit is reputed

reintroduction techniques for endangered Spanish plants. A seedbank for the conservation of the Andalusian flora is maintained by the garden and action is being taken to conserve over 20 of Andalucia's most endangered plant species. One of these is *Artemisia granatensis,* a relative of the plant used to make absinthe and which occurs only in the Sierra Nevada, where it is protected by law. The Cordoba Botanic Garden has successfully raised plants by micropropagation using tissue culture techniques and has established the species in cultivation.

Another species endemic to the Andalusian sierras of southern Spain, *Prunus ramburii,* occurs in dry montane scrub and is used locally to make an alcoholic drink. Wild populations are threatened by fire, tourism, development and a shortage of pollinators. A

to be the legendary golden apple of Greek mythology.

Another fabled tree of the Canary Islands is the Dragon Tree, *Dracaena draco*, an umbrella-shaped tree with a stout silvery grey trunk and dichotomous branches. Sword-shaped leaves are borne in dense rosettes at the ends of the branches. Small greenish-white flowers are massed in terminal panicles. The red sap, or dragon's blood, highly prized by alchemists and physicians in medieval times, has been used as a medicine, for staining violins and for embalming the dead.

Dragon's blood was a commercially valuable product in the Canary Islands and felling the trees for its extraction has been one of the main threats to wild populations of the species, which have been in decline for a long time. The species is present in five of the seven islands in the Canaries and the total population is reduced to a few hundred trees. The massive Dragon Tree at Icod, near Orotava on the north cost of Tenerife, is a major visitor attraction. The species also occurs in Cape Verde. A survey in 1996 revealed new populations in North Africa, in the Anezi region of the Anti-Atlas Mountains in Morocco. The Dragon Tree is commonly cultivated in parks and gardens in the Canary Islands and in botanic gardens elsewhere. It can be propagated from seed or from stem cuttings and reaches maturity in 30 years.

The Canary Islands have an extraordinarily rich succulent flora, with many endemic species of *Aeonium*, *Euphorbia* and *Caralluma*. Unfortunately, these are not all adequately protected in their natural habitats, and therefore ex-situ conservation is very important as an insurance against extinction.

The Viera y Clavijo Botanic Garden grows a wide range of succulents, both native and from overseas. *Euphorbia handiensis* is an endemic, found only in a small area of Fuerteventura, where it is declining as a result of development for tourism and overcollection. It can be seen growing in one of the native plant rockeries at the botanic garden, and has also been propagated using tissue culture techniques in the garden's *in vitro* cultivation laboratory.

For the past 30 years, the Viera y Clavijo Botanic Garden has been actively involved in both ex-situ and in-situ conservation, as well as helping to develop global plant conservation policy. It aims to secure a series of nature reserves on the island of Gran Canaria to cover as many as possible of the local vegetation types and endangered species, and has also recommended subsidiary local reserves throughout the islands for single local endemics such as *E. handiensis*.

The botanic gardens of Europe are many and varied and each has its unique role to play in the study and enjoyment of plant diversity. The gardens also have a historical and cultural significance of immense importance. Ranging from the world's most northerly botanic garden at Tromsø in Norway, at almost 70 degrees north, to the gardens of the Mediterranean, and with a history going back over 500 years, these gardens have been central to many historical economic events and wars. They have been equally associated with a range of colourful characters, none more so than King George III of England, who suffered intense bouts of madness and was confined to the modest Kew Palace, from where he sought calm and peace in the surrounding gardens.

Photo: BGCI

BELOW: *Asteriscus sericeus*, a species endemic to the island of Fuerteventura.

Photo: BGCI

# Chapter 4

## AFRICA

There are currently over 130 botanic gardens in Africa,
ranging from the oldest, at Durban in South Africa
and dating from 1849, to the newly restored Calabar
Botanic Garden in Nigeria. All these places are engaged
in the study, conservation and enjoyment of plants,
as well as playing an increasingly important role working
with local communities to improve their lives.

Africa is rich in diversity of habitat and species. Vegetation types include vast areas of true desert, dry bushland, wooded grassland, rainforest and montane vegetation. It is estimated that Africa has over 50,000 plant species, with a level of endemism of around 80 per cent. Many plant species have immense importance for local people and are of global significance for their timber, medicinal, food and ornamental value. The Cape flora of southern Africa is extraordinary: nearly 20 per cent of the continent's entire flora is confined to an area of around 35,000 square miles within South Africa. Throughout the continent, vegetation continues to be modified and destroyed and many plant species are threatened with extinction. From large gardens such as Kirstenbosch to small sites run by only one or two dedicated staff, Africa's botanic gardens are undergoing a renaissance and are increasingly at the forefront of initiatives aimed at sustainable development and economic progress.

# SOUTH AFRICA'S FLORAL DIVERSITY

Kirstenbosch National Botanical Garden in Cape Town, South Africa, is an internationally renowned attraction for plant lovers. Set in spectacular scenery at the foot of Table Mountain, Kirstenbosch primarily grows indigenous South African plants. It occupies an area of 528 hectares of which 36 hectares are cultivated and the remainder maintained as a nature reserve to protect the local fynbos and Afromontane forest flora. The garden was established in 1913 on land bequeathed to the nation by Cecil Rhodes. The first director of the garden was Professor Harold Pearson, who arrived in South Africa in 1903 to take up the Chair of Botany at the South African College. He agreed to be director of Kirstenbosch in an honorary capacity when the neglected estate was set aside by the Government with an annual grant of £1,000. From the outset Pearson decided that the roles of Kirstenbosch would be research, education and the preservation of natural vegetation.

Now Kirstenbosch has over 750,000 visitors each year and aims to "promote the sustainable use, conservation, appreciation and enjoyment of the exceptionally rich plant life of South Africa, for the benefit of all its people". For 50 years Kirstenbosch has been directly entrusted with the management of natural areas outside the garden: the Edith Stephens Wetland Park (3.42 hectares) on the Cape Flats, and the Tienie Versfeld Reserve (20.72 hectares) near Darling in the western Cape.

Some of the earliest plantings at Kirstenbosch were of cycads, such as *Encephalartos latifrons*. Cycads are an extraordinary group of plants related to the conifers that flourished in the time of the dinosaurs. Now only 11 genera of cycads survive, generally in small, scattered populations in tropical and subtropical parts of the world. Half the species are threatened with extinction. *Encephalartos latifrons* is critically endangered in the wild as a result of habitat loss and overcollection. Fewer than 100 plants survive and individuals are too far apart for successful pollination to occur – the beetle pollinators are thought to be extinct. The remaining plants have all been fitted with microchips to ensure that illegally collected plants can be identified. The plants in cultivation at Kirstenbosch provide an important source of material for reintroduction to the wild. A wide variety of *Encephalartos* spp. can be seen growing in the Cycad Amphitheatre at Kirstenbosch, including *E. woodii*, which is now 'Extinct in the Wild' and exists only in

Photo: Alice Notten, SANBI

botanic gardens. The plant is named after John Medley Wood, the director of the Natal Government Herbarium, who discovered the solitary male plant in Ngoya Forest in South Africa in 1895. Three of its four main stems were collected on a subsequent expedition and have been the source of all the material now grown in botanic gardens around the world. Kew received one of these stems in 1899 and the plant can still be seen growing in the Temperate House.

Kirstenbosch is part of a network of eight National Botanical Gardens (NBGs) managed by the South African National Biodiversity Institute (SANBI). SANBI was created by law in 2004 to look after the rich biodiversity of the country. This arrangement ensures that plant conservation in South Africa is truly integrated, with all aspects of ex-situ and in-situ

Photo: Adam Harrower, SANBI

PAGE 58: Cycads are highly threatened and ex-situ conservation is vital for their survival.

ABOVE: The Fynbos Walk at Kirstenbosch in early summer. The array of flowering plants includes several species of *Leucospermum*.

LEFT: Fynbos plants in spring at Kirstenbosch: *Leucadendron argenteum* (Silver Tree), *Melianthus major* (Kruidjie-roer-my-nie) and *Phylica pubescens* (Feather Bush).

The Camphor Avenue at Kirstenbosch was planted by Cecil Rhodes in 1898 along his favourite horse-riding route.

management of plants developed under the same umbrella of support. The NBGs, located in five of South Africa's nine provinces, are devoted to growing and conserving South Africa's indigenous plants, conserving over 1,350 hectares of natural vegetation and associated biodiversity within their boundaries, and to raising environmental awareness both locally and overseas. They have a vital role to play, as the Cape Floral Kingdom is one of only six worldwide and is the smallest and richest. The NBGs hold 17 per cent of South Africa's estimated 2,301 threatened plants.

Threatened species from the families Proteaceae, Amaryllidaceae, Aloaceae and Iridaceae are the best represented in the NBGs. They are mainly showy, well-known and highly attractive species that appeal to garden visitors. The botanical gardens provide biodiversity information, skills in horticulture and tourism, and support national, regional and international

Photo: Alice Notten/SANBI

natural vegetation representative of six of southern Africa's seven biome units, namely forest, fynbos, grassland, savanna, Nama Karoo, and Succulent Karoo are maintained. The only biome not represented is the desert biome, represented in Namibia almost exclusively by the Namib Desert. Collectively the gardens grow around 8,500 indigenous plant species, over one-third of South Africa's native flora.

The Karoo Desert NBG is located at the foot of the Brandwacht Mountains near Worcester, in an area with an annual rainfall of only 250mm. This garden concentrates on growing plants from the arid semi-desert areas of southern Africa, particularly the succulent species; around 2,500 succulent species are grown within the garden, including many that are very rare and under threat in the wild. One such species is *Aloe pillansii*, a tree aloe which grows up to 10m tall. In the wild *Aloe pillansii* is confined to Namibia and South Africa, and is known largely from an area in the Richtersveld. A serious decline in the wild population has reduced the numbers to around 1,000 individuals and the species has been listed as 'Critically Endangered'. There appears to be no regeneration in the wild and the older plants are dying. Baboons and porcupines damage the plants by gnawing the stems, and grazing by goats and donkeys may also be detrimental. Collectors of rare plants have also taken their toll. The few remaining wild plants provide an ecologically important source of shelter, nectar, food and moisture, particularly for birds.

The Karoo region, together with the Namib Desert, is truly remarkable for its wealth of biodiversity, with a high proportion of species found nowhere else on earth. Biologists describe the region as the Karoo-Namib centre of endemism and it is also generally known as the Succulent Karoo. This whole arid region, defined by its plant diversity, is one of the 25 global biodiversity hotspots identified by Conservation International, and the only one that is entirely arid.

The Karoo Desert National Botanical Garden has plantings that reflect the floras of different areas of the Karoo-Namib centre of endemism, such as the Richtersveld, the Knersvlakte, Tanqua Karoo and Little Karoo. There are important collections of *Haworthia*, *Conophytum* and succulent *Euphorbia* species. Approximately 11 hectares of the garden are cultivated

networks for the conservation, sustainable use and enjoyment of South Africa's flora.

In addition to Kirstenbosch, the other NBGs of South Africa are Free State, Harold Porter, Karoo Desert, Lowveld, KwaZulu-Natal, Pretoria and Walter Sisulu National Botanical Gardens. These botanic gardens, situated in different parts of the country, offer a range of climatic conditions – temperate, Mediterranean, semi-arid, subtropical and tropical. Within the gardens,

Photo: Ian Oliver/SANBI

Spring at the Karoo Desert NBG, with *Gazania krebsiana* in full flower.

and the remaining 143 hectares are managed as a reserve for the local karoo vegetation – which includes over 80 succulents. The garden provides an excellent opportunity to see succulents growing in both natural and cultivated conditions.

The influence of the National Botanical Gardens of South Africa extends far beyond their boundaries. At a national level the NBGs are very closely involved with the Botanical Society of South Africa, a non-governmental organization. The Botanical Society of South Africa was established in 1913 specifically to support the development of Kirstenbosch and now works with all the gardens in the network. The members act as the 'friends' of the gardens and support both garden-based and in-situ conservation efforts. In recent years outreach greening programmes have been developed with local communities, using indigenous plants, to 'green'

disadvantaged schools in township areas around the gardens in Cape Town, Pretoria and Johannesburg. South Africa enjoys many local cultures and languages, and the National Botanical Gardens are promoting and sharing this cultural diversity with visitors, through demonstration gardens showing how the different cultures use South Africa's indigenous plants. The Karoo Desert NBG, for example, has a display area with a traditional cooking shelter typical of the arid Richtersveld area.

South Africa's NBGs have also helped support other gardens in southern Africa through the Southern African Botanical Diversity Network (SABONET) Programme. This aimed at upgrading facilities and strengthening the level of botanical diversity expertise throughout the subcontinent. The participating countries are Angola, Botswana, Lesotho, Malawi, Mozambique, Namibia, South Africa, Swaziland, Zambia and Zimbabwe.

# GARDENS OF THE RAINFOREST

The Limbe Botanical and Zoological Gardens in Cameroon is one of the most important gardens in Africa's rainforest region. Limbe is a coastal town situated at the foot of Mount Cameroon, the highest mountain in West and Central Africa (4,095m) and an area of outstanding biodiversity. The botanic garden was established in 1892 by the German colonial administration and, in common with other early tropical botanic gardens, it was developed as a centre for agricultural plant research. Cash crops such as cocoa, coffee, sugar cane, rubber and banana were introduced into Cameroon and other German colonies through the botanic garden at Limbe, influencing the agricultural development and economies of many tropical African countries.

From the outset, the garden's infrastructure provided accommodation, laboratories, a library and herbarium to support research, and offered classrooms for teaching agricultural and horticultural students. Later, during a phase of British colonial administration, technical expertise was provided by the Royal Botanic Gardens, Kew. From the 1970s, Cameroon's newly created agricultural and forestry institutions took over most of the research and teaching functions of Limbe Botanic Garden and the garden experienced a period of neglect. Farming, rubbish dumping, soil excavation and the building of private houses took place within the grounds. The laboratory became a hospital and later a hotel, and the garden's headquarters were shared with other government services. Fortunately, local concern led to improvements in the 1980s, and British technical and financial assistance were provided to restore the garden. New roles were identified for the botanic garden and its current aims are to support the sustainable use of the forest by the local population as a practical means of conservation; to encourage scientific studies of biodiversity; to educate community groups on caring for the environment; and to promote tourism and recreation.

The gardens cover a stunning landscape of 52 hectares featuring two hills, a central lowland with a wetland area, and an important river running throughout its length. Different areas are being developed to display the different habitat types: lowland evergreen rainforest, maritime, wetland and riverine forests. Plant species used for medicine, fruit, timber, dyes and spices are displayed. Cameroon is currently one of the leading exporters of timber in the Congo Basin, and the garden contains important hardwood species including Moabi (*Baillonella toxisperma*), Bubinga (*Guibourtia tessmanni*), Wenge (*Milletia laurentii*), Zebrawood (*Microberlinia bisulcata*) and Ironwood (*Lophira alata*).

Unsustainable logging and shifting cultivation are two of the threats to Cameroon's rich forests. Limbe is helping to tackle the impact of shifting cultivation through education designed to complement the activities of the agricultural services. A model crop farm has been developed in the garden to demonstrate improved farming practices, such as crop association and rotation, agroforestry techniques and the use of composting and mulching. Environmental education is also taken out to the villages with discussion meetings organized to promote the importance of, and explain changes to, the forest ecosystem. Emphasis is put on teaching children to become more responsible and environmentally friendly towards the forest. Similar contacts are organized in urban areas, to gain the understanding of people who have moved to the towns but may still influence rural communities through their frequent visits back to their villages. Urban carpenters are encouraged to obtain timber from sustainable forestry sources.

Limbe is helping to develop village tree nurseries to provide alternatives for the rural community, increase income and reduce pressure on the forest. Beekeeping courses are also organized for some of the young people from villages around the forest; modern techniques in honey production have resulted in both improved quality and increased productivity. By collaborating with local schools, and providing planting materials to develop school gardens, the botanic garden is promoting responsibility for management of the environment.

Two complementary rainforest reserves are managed in association with the garden. One (covering 143 square miles) is on Mount Cameroon – an area of huge biodiversity importance with at least 45 endemic plant species. The other (of 14 square miles) is on already degraded lowland forest that is being partly enriched to form a living gene bank. The garden lies between these

An avenue of tropical trees (*Pimenta racemosa*) at Limbe Botanic Garden.

two reserves, and facilities within it have been developed to provide an institutional base from which scientists can study the reserves.

The richly forested Democratic Republic of Congo (formerly known as Zaire) has two main botanic gardens, both created in 1900. Both gardens have herbaria and libraries and have the potential to be centres of research, education and conservation. At present the Kisantu Botanic Garden, situated in the lower Zaire region, 75 miles from Kinshasa, undertakes research in arboriculture and is involved in trials for useful plant species. This botanic garden was created by the Jesuit, Frère Justin Gillet. It has an area of 225 hectares, including 100 hectares of Frère Gillet's original garden, and has about 3,000 species in cultivation. Included in the grounds of Kisantu is an arboretum with around 200 native tree species, a Palmetum, succulent greenhouse, orchid collection and collections of medicinal, fruit and other useful plants.

The Kisantu Botanic Garden has recently been involved in a project to conserve and increase the number of edible caterpillars available to local people. Caterpillar meat provides a valuable source of protein within the region but in some areas caterpillars are becoming scarce because of changes to local management of the forest. Research has been undertaken on the preferred food plants of edible species and guidance is given to villagers on where to plant suitable trees and harvest caterpillars sustainably.

The National Botanic Garden of Belgium provided assistance with this project, helping to prepare and store herbarium specimens of the caterpillar food plants.

The development of the Botanic Garden of Eala at Mbandaka, in the equatorial region of the Democratic Republic of Congo, was largely due to the Belgian Professor E. Laurent from Gembloux. The garden covers an area of approximately 370 hectares, with special collections (125 hectares), forest reserve (190 hectares), marshland (50 hectares) and savanna (7 hectares). Sadly, the garden has suffered from neglect, with limited maintenance and unplanned felling of trees. Nevertheless, it holds an estimated 5,000 plant species, nearly all of which are native to the country.

The rich diversity of native wild plants throughout Africa is a resource of great importance for rural communities. Wild plants are, for example, essential for primary healthcare throughout Africa. In Ghana, as elsewhere on the continent, up to 80 per cent of the population relies on medicinal plants sourced in the wild. With the demise of the forests, however, communities find it increasingly hard to source their medicinal plants, and practitioners must travel ever greater distances to collect them. Created over a century ago, on a site that had been used as a health resort for convalescent colonial officers, Aburi Botanic Garden has been helping to improve communities' access to medicinal plants, and to encourage their sustainable use. Within the garden a 20-hectare model Medicinal Plant Garden has been created, with plantings based on surveys to find out what the local communities use for healthcare. The garden was planted with 1,361 medicinal plant seedlings, and a plant nursery established to hold 5,000 more. Lectures, seminars and workshops are held for herbalists on how to propagate and cultivate medicinal plants. The garden is also used to encourage communities to set up their own nurseries and first aid gardens.

These activities have been accompanied by the publication of two manuals on medicinal plants, one on harvesting, preparation and storage, and the other on propagation. Aburi also provides communities with seedlings (over two million to date), and is involved in complementary activities, such as the enhancement of schools, churchyards, towns and villages, promotion of some traditional medicinal plant management systems, and the management of protected areas.

# GARDENS IN EAST AFRICA

In Kenya, Nairobi Arboretum has great value as a green lung for the rapidly growing city with a population of around 3 million. Consisting of 30 hectares of wooded landscape situated about two miles from the city centre and adjacent to the State House, Nairobi Arboretum is one of that city's few remaining green spaces, with shaded walkways, picnic lawns and jogging trails.

The Arboretum was first established in 1907 by Mr Batiscombe, then Deputy Conservator of Forests, to try out introduced forestry trees for Kenya. It was declared a national reserve in 1932 and in 1996 became a publicly owned reserve. Following a period of neglect during the 1970s and 1980s, the Arboretum has enjoyed a new lease of life since the establishment of the Friends of Nairobi Arboretum (FONA) in 1993, as a project of the historic East Africa Natural History Society. The Arboretum has over 350 species of indigenous and exotic trees. The diverse vegetation is also home to over 100 species of birds, populations of both Sykes and Vervet Monkeys, a wide variety of butterflies and other small wildlife.

Kenya has more than 800 indigenous tree species.

Trees which grow naturally in the highland forests of the Aberdare Range are particularly well represented in the Nairobi Arboretum. Dominant members of the Nairobi dry evergreen-deciduous forests which grow abundantly at the Arboretum include *Croton megalocarpus*, *Brachylaena huillensis*, *Podocarpus falcatus* and *Markhamia lutea*. *Croton megalocarpus,* known as Mukinduri in the Kikuyu language, is the logo of FONA, and over 300 mature trees grow within the grounds. *Brachylaena huillensis* is a hardwood species whose timber is heavily exploited in the wood-carving industries in Kenya and Tanzania. A few fine specimens of Mvuli, *Milicia excelsa*, remain from early plantings. This tree has attractive timber for quality furniture and is widely traded as Iroko; it was extensively used by early European settlers in East Africa and also harvested for export. It is now overexploited in Kenya, only a few trees remaining in moist forests such as Kakamega and Shimba Hills. Red Stinkwood, *Prunus africana* (known widely as African Cherry) was a quality timber tree exported from Kenya in the past but today it is better known for the medicinal properties of its bark, which is used to treat prostate problems.

Developing a collection of succulent plants at Nairobi Botanic Garden.

Photo: Andrew McRobb/Board of Trustees of the Royal Botanic Gardens, Kew

Other botanic gardens in Kenya include the Nairobi Botanic Garden, established in 1997, which is associated with the National Museums of Kenya and houses East Africa's leading herbarium, and gardens associated with the Universities of Maseno, Moi and Egerton. Elsewhere in the region, Tanzania has three botanic gardens, the oldest being Dar es Salaam Botanic Garden, established in 1893. In Uganda, Entebbe Botanical Gardens are situated on the northern shores of Lake Victoria. The gardens were laid out in 1898 by Mr Whyte, the first curator, and now occupy about 35 hectares. The main role of the garden was initially to serve as a reception centre for plants of potential economic value to Uganda, and at one time the collection consisted of 2,500 species of plants of tropical, sub-tropical and warm temperature zones. After a period of deterioration due to Uganda's political turmoil, Entebbe Botanic Garden is now attempting to restore its infrastructure and collections, concentrating its efforts on education, conservation and research with identification of species, and the cultivation of threatened indigenous species such as Yams (*Dioscorea* spp) and wild rice.

# ISLAND GARDENS IN THE INDIAN OCEAN

The islands of the Indian Ocean are a fascinating blend of African and Asian influences, with the traditional crops in the villages reflecting this cultural mix. The botanic gardens of the region reflect both the history of later colonialism and the current need to protect fragile island floras.

### THE MASCARENES

Mauritius, Rodrigues, and Réunion make up the Mascarene Islands and are of great botanical importance. Indeed, the first botanic garden in the tropics was the Royal Botanic Garden, Pamplemousses, established on Mauritius in 1735. Originally developed to boost colonial income through plantation crops, this lush tropical garden with many historical and ornamental features is now involved in the conservation of the threatened island flora. Since 1987 the garden has been known as the Sir Seewoosagur Ramgoolam Botanic Garden, named after the first prime minister of Mauritius.

The volcanic island of Réunion is located approximately 90 miles west of Mauritius and 485 miles east of Madagascar. It has a great diversity of vegetation types, ranging from littoral vegetation and lowland semi-dry forest to rainforest, cloudforest, and heath vegetation on the highest summits of Piton des Neiges (3,069m) and Piton de la Fournaise (2,631m), a still active volcano. The native flora includes around 240 fern species and more than 500 flowering plant species, about 160 of which are endemic to the island. Many of the native plants are in need of conservation and are being cared for by the Conservatoire Botanique National de Mascarin (CBNM). Created in 1986, this 12.5-hectare garden is located at an elevation of 500m, on the leeward side of La Réunion, above the town of Saint-Leu. Réunion is an overseas *département* of France and the Conservatoire belongs to the French network of eight National Botanical Conservatories which study and conserve the French flora.

Initially, the main goal of CBNM was ex-situ conservation. Now, with 60 per cent of the endangered flora of Réunion successfully rescued and established in cultivation in the garden, CBNM is becoming more involved in the management and monitoring of species and populations in their natural habitats. Permanent plots have been established in the rainforest for long-term study of plant diversity and vegetation dynamics; field surveys are carried out to monitor the rare endemic plants; and natural areas of high conservation value are assessed for their protection or sustainable management. Recovery programmes have been established for species such as *Lomatophyllum macrum*, using material grown in the garden. Another important aspect of work is the study and control of invasive plants which have a devastating effect on the native flora of all the Mascarene Islands. CBMN is drawing up a Green List

OPPOSITE TOP:
*Hyophorbe amaricaulis* is known from only one surviving plant in the wild. It is currently being propagated using tissue culture techniques by the Royal Botanic Gardens, Kew, with Mauritius Botanic Garden.

OPPOSITE BOTTOM:
The indigenous flora of many Indian Ocean islands is under threat from introduced, non-native species. Among the more aggressive is *Heliconia psittacorum*, shown here.

of native and endemic plants for replanting on a wider scale in urban areas, as an alternative to the cultivation of potential or known invasive species, and in order to reduce pressure on plants in the wild.

The endemic plants of Rodrigues have suffered a fate shared by many small oceanic island floras, all but two of the species being listed as either 'Extinct' or 'Endangered'. At the time of early colonization in 1691, this small island of 42 square miles, lying 357 miles east of Mauritius, was covered in forest and described as a paradise on earth. Now the landscape supports cultivated crops, rough pasture and eroded hillsides. Fortunately, the island is the home of one of the most celebrated plant conservation success stories involving international collaboration between botanic gardens. Bois Papaya, *Badula balfouriana*, is a critically endangered tree species endemic to Rodrigues. The leaves and bark of Bois Papaya have been used in traditional medicine to relieve teething problems in infants and young children. Now there are fewer than ten known individuals growing in the wild on Rodrigues. Measures have been taken to increase the population of this species in its natural habitat; ten to twelve individuals, grown from seed or propagated by cuttings, have been planted in the upland Grande Montagne, one of the remnants of the Rodriguan upland native forest, by the Mauritian Wildlife Foundation in collaboration with the Ministry for Rodrigues Forestry Service.

In 1982 a cutting was taken from one of the wild trees and established in cultivation at the Conservatoire Botanique National de Brest in France. Four new plants were produced by cuttings from the original plant in 2000. *B. balfouriana* has also been in cultivation at the Botanic Garden in Copenhagen, Denmark, since 1985. Three plants were grown from seed collected in two expeditions in 1985 and 1987, on the slopes of Grande Montagne. One was subsequently lost and neither of the two remaining plants has yet produced seeds. In addition, an individual plant produced by a cutting in Brest was sent to Copenhagen in 2004 and a micropropagated plant of one of the two Copenhagen clones was sent to Brest. Micropropagation has recently made it possible to produce a large number of plants in an all-year-round process without seasonal dependency. These plants may be used in seed orchards, for cuttings, and ultimately further reintroduction into the wild.

Photo: V. Sarrasin/Board of Trustees of the Royal Botanic Gardens, Kew

Photo: BGCI

Photo: Peter Wyse Jackson

The Coco-de-mer, which grows naturally in the Seychelles, is a species of palm and has the largest seeds of any plant. It is listed as 'Vulnerable' in the wild.

## THE SEYCHELLES

The National Botanic Garden of the Seychelles provides an oasis of green shade. The century-old Botanic Garden is situated at the south end of the capital, Victoria, on the island of Mahe. Covering six hectares, the gardens are planted with a wide variety of indigenous and exotic trees, including the Seychelles' unique Coco-de-mer palms. The orchid garden is particularly attractive. Visitors to the garden can also see Flying Foxes and the giant Aldabra Land Tortoise. The Seychelles are made up of over a hundred small islands, of which some are composed of granite and others are coralline. The garden is actively involved in the conservation of the country's unique flora and is a key partner in the recently developed national strategy for plant conservation, a response to the Global Strategy for Plant Conservation.

## MADAGASCAR

The island of Madagascar has an extraordinary diversity of plants and animals and is considered to be one of the top global priorities for biodiversity conservation. The world's fourth largest island, lying in the Indian Ocean, 250 miles from southern Africa, has a unique natural and cultural heritage. The plants and animals have evolved in relative isolation, since the separation of Madagascar from the ancient land mass of Gondwanaland, approximately 65 million years ago. The island's dramatic escarpments, mountain ranges and a central plateau area, together with more gentle foothills and coastal plains, support an equally diverse flora with more than 80 per cent of Madagascar's plant species being endemic to the island.

Madagascar has a remarkable succulent plant flora with over 600 species, most of which are endemic. Sadly, around 80 per cent of the original vegetation of the island of Madagascar has been destroyed and many species are threatened with extinction. The spiny desert of the south is perhaps the most amazing of all. In a small coastal region about 30 miles wide an extraordinary dryland vegetation, made up of succulent *Euphorbia* spp. and plants of the endemic Didiereaceae family, subsists on thin skeletal soils. The four genera of the Didiereaceae family are all confined to the south and southwest of the island. The closest relatives of this family are the Cactaceae, plants of the Didiereaceae sometimes being known as the cacti of the old world.

All species of the Didiereaceae are threatened, however, because of the vulnerability of the spiny forest habitat, which is being cleared, primarily for subsistence agriculture. Another threat to the Didiereaceae has been commercial collection of wild plants for sale to succulent plant enthusiasts in Europe, Japan and the USA. In an effort to control this trade the entire family is listed on Appendix II of CITES. Monitoring of trade under the terms of CITES helped to stop the import of many thousands of wild-collected specimens of the Didiereaceae into Europe during the 1980s. The plants were claimed to be propagated in nurseries but this was shown to be untrue and increased efforts were taken to stop the illegal trade.

There are some protected areas to conserve the natural habitats of the Didiereaceae, such as the Strict Nature Reserve of Tsimanampetsota, which protects *Alluaudia procera* and other succulent species. Ex-situ conservation is also an urgent priority, given the scale of destruction of the natural habitat. The Arboretum d'Antsokay in Tuléar, Madagascar, is a remarkable botanic garden dedicated to the display and conservation of Madagascar's unique succulent plant flora. Founded by Hermann Petignat and his Malagasy wife Simone in 1980, the garden is now run by their son, Andry Petignat. There are about 540 species growing in the collection, including all the Didiereaceae and the critically endangered *Aloe suzannae.*

The main botanic garden in Madagascar is the Parc Botanique et Zoologique de Tsimbazaza in the capital city of Antananarivo. Established in 1925, the garden is situated along the artificial lake of Tsimbazaza, which was created by King Radama in 1815. During the 19th century the lake was a site for promenading and for occasional sacrifices of Zebu cattle. The garden is now a good place to see Madagascan endemics such as the orchid *Angraecum sesquipedale*, which has huge waxy yellowish flowers up to 12cm across with a very long spur extending to 40cm. The flowers are highly fragrant at night. This species is threatened with extinction in the wild but is now well established in cultivation around the world. Also of note in the garden are the Madagascan Periwinkle, *Catharanthus rosea*, renowned for its role in the treatment of Hodgkinson's disease, and endemic palms such as *Chrysalidocarpus madagascariensis.*

Botanic gardens play a vital role in preventing the extinction of plant species on the oceanic islands off the coast of Africa. With so many endemic plants and competing pressures on the land, gardens increasingly provide a refuge which cannot always be guaranteed in the wild. In the countries of Africa itself, gardens are responding more and more to the challenge of biodiversity conservation whilst at the same time ensuring that biodiversity benefits rural populations to the full. Africa's network of botanic gardens and arboreta needs to be maintained, restored and expanded so that these needs can be met.

*Alluadia procera* is one of eleven species of Madagascar's succulent Didiereaceae family, characteristic of the unique spiny forest vegetation.

The historic lake and botanic garden of Tsimbazaza in the capital city of Madagascar, Antananarivo.

# Chapter 5

## ASIA

Gardens in Asia – both west and east – have an
ancient tradition. The earliest gardens of Babylon, Persia
and China were probably hunting reserves, but carefully
designed gardens are known from around 2000 BC. Elements
of oriental gardens are replicated as ornamental features
in modern botanic gardens across the globe, and some
of the oldest gardens in the world survive in Asia, where
they have been maintained and renewed.

Asia has a magnificent diversity of botanic gardens, many with their origins in the very earliest garden traditions of the orient. There are now over 200 botanic gardens in east and southeast Asia, with over 100 in China and more than 50 in Japan. These gardens combine ancient features of garden design with cutting-edge botanical science. Increasingly, gardens throughout Asia are responding to the challenge of plant conservation in an age of rapid economic growth and infrastructural development. Many are working together to help stem the loss of plant diversity in a range of habitats and landscape types, from arid steppes to tropical rainforests.

# CHINA

Within China, new botanic gardens continue to be developed at this time of rapid growth in prosperity. The Chinese Academy of Sciences and the Beijing municipal government, for example, are currently planning to build a new national botanical garden, which will be combined with the existing Beijing Botanical Garden, established in 1956.

Throughout China, botanic gardens are important for recreation within their urban settings, as well as for plant exploration, research and conservation. China has a rich floral diversity, with ten per cent of the world's total flora, and native plants are of major significance in providing resources for shelter, nutrition and healthcare, as well as ornamental plants of cultural importance. Certain species have been cultivated in China since ancient times. The chrysanthemum and peony have long been symbols of beauty, and China's natural wealth of native ornamental plants has contributed to the gardens of the west since the 16th century; the intrepid plant hunter, George Forrest, contributed greatly to British gardening through his introductions of camellias, gentians, lilies, magnolias, and primulas, many of which were collected during his travels in China. Based at the Royal Botanic Garden, Edinburgh, Forrest undertook seven plant-collecting expeditions between 1910 and 1932, following in the footsteps of earlier collectors such as Père Jean Pierre Armand David, who discovered 250 new species of plant.

One of the many species indigenous to China that are now well-established garden plants in temperate areas around the world is *Davidia involucrata*, the Handkerchief or Dove Tree, discovered by Père David in 1869 and introduced into western cultivation by Ernest Wilson in 1904. The monospecific genus, native only to China, is considered a relict of the Tertiary flora and is of considerable scientific interest. It is also a beautiful tree, prized for its distinctive flowers. Occurring in montane or cloudforest with a cool humid climate, the species is now considered to be 'Vulnerable', overcollection from wild populations having reduced its natural regeneration.

Magnolias are a group of horticulturally important plants that have a natural centre of diversity in China. *Magnolia delavayi* is a large, evergreen, temperate shrub or tree growing to about 10m, with fragrant, cup-shaped white flowers. Confined in the wild to the provinces of Sichuan and Yunnan, *Magnolia delavayi* is considered to be 'Endangered' in its natural habitats. It has, however, been grown for centuries in China, and in Yunnan there are specimens which are at least 800 years old. This magnolia is now becoming increasingly popular in cultivation in the west – particularly the new red forms.

Other Chinese species of the Magnoliaceae are being conserved through an international programme of the Global Trees Campaign. Scientists at the Kunming Botanic Garden are working with Fauna & Flora International to

Photo: Howard Rice

PAGE 72: Kyoto Botanic Garden, Japan.

LEFT: Originally from China, the Handkerchief Tree is now grown widely in temperate gardens across the world.

Bamboo in the famous medicinal gardens at Kunming.

conserve five species in their natural habitats. *Magnolia sargentiana* is a horticulturally important deciduous species from Sichuan and northeast Yunnan. Only large trees are known to remain in the wild. Surveys are being undertaken for this and four other species as a basis for planning conservation action in their natural habitats.

## RESEARCH AND CONSERVATION

The importance of botanic gardens for research, biodiversity conservation, education and the development and utilization of plant resources is recognized at a national level by the Chinese Academy of Sciences, which has responsibility for a core network of 15 gardens managed fully or in part by the Academy. These gardens collectively grow over half the native plants in China.

The Kunming Botanical Garden is renowned worldwide and is a haven for plant enthusiasts. The province of Yunnan in which it occurs has about four per cent of the land area of China and over 50 per cent of the plant diversity. There is a tremendous range of different natural

habitats within Yunnan which helps to explain its diverse flora. The Kunming Botanical Garden has very important collections of camellias including nearly 70 species and over 100 cultivars of *Camellia reticulata*; a collection of over 300 species and cultivars of *Rhododendron*; and the famed Magnolia Garden with 90 species of the Magnoliaceae. As well as conserving rare *Magnolia* spp., Kunming has a major conservation programme for other rare and threatened tree species of Yunnan.

Situated in the bend of the Luosuo River, a tributary of the Mekong, is another important botanic garden of Yunnan, Xishuangbanna Tropical Botanical Garden. Significant areas of rainforest remain within the garden, whose principal aims are the conservation and sustainable use of plant diversity, as well as the preservation of ethnic culture and improvement of rural livelihoods.

Wuhan, strategically situated in the centre of China, on the river Yangtze, is China's fifth largest city, with a history spanning 3,500 years. The bustle of downtown Hankou, one of the three towns that make up the Wuhan conurbation, is in sharp contrast with the surroundings of

Photo: BGCI

A classic view of Wuhan Botanic Garden, which has an important research and conservatiion function.

East Lake. The lake itself covers approximately 13 square miles, and the Wuhan Botanic Garden is situated on its shore. The garden was established in 1956 as a national resource and research centre for Hubei Province, which has a rich, distinctive flora. The garden is attracting increasing numbers of visitors, with its magnificent glasshouse displays of chrysanthemums and illuminated water-gardens. Behind the scenes Wuhan is a very important research and biodiversity conservation centre. The garden covers an area of 70 hectares and houses within it the world's largest genetic pool of kiwifruit, a genus with its centre of diversity in Hubei, and the largest collection of aquatic plants in east Asia. The garden also has two satellite gardens, the Three Gorges Botanical Garden in Yichang City and the Rare and Endangered Plant Transition Preservation Site in Huangpi District. Wuhan Botanic Garden maintains a documented and labelled collection of 7,000 plant species to support its research and conservation functions.

Shanghai Botanical Garden has enjoyed a period of expansion in recent years, receiving millions of visitors each year, and it is known especially for its ornamental plant displays, especially bonsai plants. A magnificent greenhouse has been constructed recently. It consists of two smaller greenhouses, one for tropical rainforest plants and the other for succulent plants displayed against a backdrop of desert scenes. The current Shanghai Botanical Garden is surrounded by buildings and has no room for further expansion. A new Botanic Garden is therefore being developed – the Chenshan Botanical Garden, situated in suburban Songjiang District, 11 miles west of the city. This new garden, which aims to be an internationally renowned centre of horticulture and conservation expertise, will cover 210 hectares, an area three and a half times that of the existing garden.

## HONG KONG

Development pressures in China are huge, as the country experiences rapid economic growth, and botanic gardens have a key role to play in remedial plant conservation. The Kadoorie Farm and Botanic Garden in

Photo: BGCI

The propagation area at Kadoorie Garden Farm, Hong Kong.

peak. Kadoorie Farm was established in the 1950s to improve local rural livelihoods through agricultural research and assistance. At the same time the farm developed another role, as a centre for horticulture, with attractive botanic gardens developed on the original degraded rocky slopes of the site. By the 1990s agriculture had declined in Hong Kong and a new focus for the Kadoorie Farm was needed. A report by the Royal Botanic Gardens, Kew, suggested a new emphasis – biodiversity conservation.

Kadoorie Farm and Botanic Garden provides a natural sanctuary for Hong Kong's native mammals, with wild boar, Barking Deer, Chinese Porcupines and Styan's Squirrels all found within the cultivated and wild areas. Less common sightings include Leopard Cats, Chinese Pangolins and Masked Palm Civets. Conservation of the local flora has always been part of the work of Kadoorie, with particular emphasis on the native orchids. Hong Kong has 123 native orchid species, 100 of which grow at Kadoorie; some of these are planted as part of the orchid conservation programme and others grow naturally among the rocks and on the trunks of trees. Orchid Haven is a display area, with propagation facilities for the most endangered species. The demand from overseas for Chinese orchids has put pressure on some of the attractive and naturally rare species which have been traded from mainland China through Hong Kong. Kadoorie advises the Government on dealing with the illegal trade in wild orchids and provides a rescue centre for confiscated plants. Orchid conservation work also includes the propagation of globally 'Endangered' *Paphiopedilum* spp., studies of orchids in their natural habitats in the limestone regions of Yunnan, Guizhou and Guangxi, and help in conservation planning and assessments of Hong Kong's rich indigenous orchid flora.

Hong Kong has expanded its mission since 2003 to minimize the loss of biodiversity and promote sustainability in the southern Chinese provinces of Guangdong, Guangxi and Hainan. The China Programme of Kadoorie Farm and Botanic Garden is working with a wide range of partners, including local government, forest departments, nature reserve managers and academic institutions.

Situated in Hong Kong's central New Territories, a short distance away from thriving downtown Hong Kong, Kadoorie Farm nestles beneath Tai Mo Shan (Goddess of Mercy Mountain), the territory's highest

China has a long tradition of using plants for medicinal purposes. Plants are still largely collected from the wild, and this has led to various species becoming threatened with extinction. In an attempt to remedy this problem, the botanic gardens of China pay particular attention to the conservation of medicinal plants. With this in mind, the Guangxi Botanical Garden of Medicinal Plants, in the eastern suburbs of Nanning, was established in 1959, principally to collect, cultivate and study Chinese medicinal plants.

# JAPAN: STYLE AND SYMBOLISM

Gardens in Japan represent a very long cultural heritage, the creation of gardens being considered a major art form, reflecting the importance of nature. The essential components of a Japanese garden include various forms of stone, sand, water and individually placed plants, composed in a stylized arrangement. The individual stones, often chosen to represent mountains, are chosen with great care, their degree of erosion having symbolic significance. In the dry garden of Zen Buddhism, stone can be used to represent water, as can the raked surface of sand in gardens traditionally used for contemplation by scholars, nobles and monks. Plants traditionally associated with Japanese gardens include pines and mosses cultivated as ornamentals. Among the most famous of the Japanese traditional gardens are the Golden and Silver Pavilions of Kyoto. Kyoto was the country's capital from 794 to 1603, and has an outstanding array of ancient sanctuaries and gardens; the Kyoto Prefecture Botanical Garden currently has the largest living collection of plants held by a Japanese botanical garden, with 12,000 species.

The first botanic garden in Japan was established in the Edo period. In 1638, Miyakuen, which means the medicinal garden, was created by the Tokugawa feudal government. It was moved to its current location in Tokyo in 1684 and became the Botanic Garden of the University of Tokyo in 1879. All the other botanic gardens of Japan were developed after the Meiji era (1868–1912), when Japan was eager to absorb Western culture and knowledge. Sixteen botanic gardens were established during this time and a second major period of botanic garden development took place in the years after 1960.

The majority of Japanese botanic gardens are relatively small, with the smaller gardens being predominantly glasshouses or medicinal school gardens. The largest garden is Kobe City Forest Plant Garden, which covers an area of 42.6 hectares. Most of the botanic gardens have a public amenity or tourism function rather than a major research role, but Japanese gardens are playing an increasingly active role in conservation. The Botanic Garden of Toyko University has a significant role in caring for the Japanese flora,

Makino Kochi Prefectural Botanic Garden, Japan. One of his country's greatest botanists, Tomitaro Makino (1862–1957) gave scientific names to 2,500 of the 6,000 plants that are endemic to Japan.

Photo: BGCI

Japan 79

Photo: BGCI

The Iris Garden at Kyoto Botanic Garden.

damage to the natural ecosystems. Grazing by escaped livestock and the illegal collection of plants have also been significant threats to the flora. An emergency survey carried by the Environment Agency (now Ministry of Environment – MOE) in 1985 showed that 80 species, about half the endemic species of the Bonin Islands, were on the brink of extinction. The Bonin Rare Plants Recovery Project is undertaken by the MOE in cooperation with other institutions and targets 11 species: *Melastoma tetramerum*, *Rhododendron boninense*, *Calanthe hattori*, *Calanthe hoshii*, *Pittosporum parvifolium*, *Calicanthe nishimura*, *Piper postelsianum*, *Asplenium cardiophyllum*, *Malaxsis boninensis*, *Luisia boninensis*, and *Cirrhopetalum boninense*. In addition to research and monitoring, plants cultivated at the botanic garden are reintroduced to the wild where the remaining populations have seriously lost their viability. The project has been very successful in species cultivation, but not as satisfactory in reintroduction. However, it has been reported recently that some individuals of *Melastoma tetramerum*, which were raised from the one remaining tree and reintroduced into its natural habitat, have now become established in the wild.

and in recent years has been involved in an intensive species recovery project in the Bonin Islands. The Bonin Islands, about 620 miles south of Tokyo, consist of about 30 small islands with an extremely rich endemic flora and fauna. Unfortunately, agricultural development and deforestation, which began in the 19th century when the islands were first settled, have caused heavy

# KOREA

The Korean peninsula has around 3,000 vascular plant species, with about 400 endemics, half of which are restricted to South Korea. The main facility for plant conservation in Korea is the National Arboretum, formerly the Kwangnung Arboretum, in an area of natural forest that has been preserved since 1468 as part of the estate attached to the tomb of King Sejo.

The arboretum has 15 display gardens, including a Forest Museum and small wildlife conservation facility. One of the three departments of the Arboretum is now devoted to conservation work. To link together the work of all the botanic gardens, arboreta and herbaria in

Korea, the arboretum has developed a National Plant Database System, which will document all the holdings of both living germplasm and herbarium specimens in the country.

The arboretum works closely with the Korean Association of Botanical Gardens and Arboreta, which includes 14 national and public gardens, 12 private gardens and five university-owned gardens, as well as supporting the development of new gardens in Korea. The Korean Association works with overseas gardens such as Royal Botanic Gardens, Kew, and with BGCI to develop an integrated approach to conservation, combining both in-situ and ex-situ approaches.

# SINGAPORE: TIMBER, SPICES AND MEDICINAL PLANTS

The Singapore Botanic Gardens is one the world's best known botanic gardens. Established on their present site in 1859, the gardens were developed to cultivate plants that reflect the importance of spices to the local economy. Singapore was originally founded as a trading centre, spices being the most important item of trade. Part of the land on which the gardens now stand had previously been cultivated and part was covered with pristine rainforest. The remnant patch of rainforest still forms part of the garden today, with 314 native plant species surviving in the four-hectare forest patch. This compares well with the diversity of the Bukit Timah Nature Reserve, which covers 70 hectares and has 900 species recorded.

The canopy trees of the remnant rainforest in the botanic garden grow to over 50m tall and include representatives of Singapore's original timber trees: Jelutong, *Dyera costulata*, *Koompassia malaccensis*, *Terminalia subspathulata* and the dipterocarps *Shorea gratissima*, *Shorea leprosula*, *S. macroptera*, *S. pauciflora*, and *S. ovalis* are some of the magnificent trees that grow there. Other valuable plants include Agarwood, *Aquilaria malaccensis*, which produces a valuable incense; rattans belonging to the palm genera *Calamus*, *Daemonorops* and *Korthalsia*; many local fruit trees and medicinal plants, such as *Eurycoma longifolia*, *Labisia pumila*, *Scaphium linearicarpum* and *S. macropodum*. The two *Scaphium* spp. are both called Kembang Semangkok (fill-a-cup) in Malay, as a fruit left in a little water for a short while will spectacularly fill the cup with its mucilage, which is used as medicine for coughs, asthma, dysentery and fever. Another of the rainforest medicinal species is *Calophyllum lanigerum* var. *austrocoriaceus*, which has recently been identified as a possible treatment against the HIV virus.

The structure and floristic composition of the remnant forest have inevitably been modified; the canopy structure has been broken up following the death of

Recreating the rainforest environment in Singapore Botanic Garden.

Photo: BGCI

Replicas of giant club-mosses within the recently established Evolution Garden at Singapore Botanic Garden.

emergent trees, which has encouraged the growth of climbers and hindered the regeneration of canopy species. The planting of aggressive exotics has also caused problems; there are now 80 introduced species established in the rainforest, the most aggressive of which are herbs, such as *Costus lucanusianum*, *Heliconia psittacorum* and *Thaumatococcus danielli*; climbers, such as *Dioscorea sansibarensis*, *Thunbergia grandiflora* and *Tanaecium jaroba*; and trees, such as *Castilla elastica*. Squirrel populations are also a problem in the rainforest fragment and may be a factor in low regeneration rates. The botanic garden is actively managing and restoring its precious rainforest, the first step being a long-term monitoring programme to count

the trees and follow their flowering, fruiting and regeneration patterns. The rehabilitation process involves the removal of exotics, control of climbers, collection and the germination of seed for enrichment planting and the restoration of a complete canopy layer. Ripe seed collected from the rainforest plants is grown in a plant nursery before being carefully planted out to fill forest gaps. Enrichment planting helps to increase the population size of very rare tree species, such as *Memecylon cantleyi*, known only in Singapore from the two plants in the botanic garden's rainforest.

*Borassodendron machadonis* is a special case of an exotic, an extremely rare palm from central and north peninsular Malaysia, where it is known from only about five populations. It was introduced into the Singapore Botanic Gardens early in the twentieth century and fruits regularly. Over the years, the fallen fruits have been conveniently disposed of by being thrown into the adjacent rainforest, where they have become established. So, almost by accident, this plant has been conserved within the botanic garden and hopefully from there it can be relocated back into the wild.

The Singapore Botanic Gardens provide an invaluable green haven close to the bustle of the city centre, attracting over two million visitors each year, more than half of whom are from overseas. Behind the scenes, the gardens are a regional hub of scientific activity. The permanent collection of herbarium specimens was established in 1875 and continues to provide one of the most important centres for plant taxonomic research and biodiversity research in southeast Asia.

The garden's early reputation as a world centre for tropical botany and its economic application was established by the first director, Henry Nicholas Ridley, popularly known as Mad Ridley or Rubber Ridley. As well as promoting tropical agriculture, Ridley was an ardent field botanist who travelled throughout peninsular Malaysia and the Indonesian archipelago. He was keenly aware of the need to conserve tropical rainforests and their biodiversity, alongside the development of rubber and palm oil, which he also helped to establish as an Asian plantation crop.

# MALAYSIA: TROPICAL FOREST

Within peninsular Malaysia, one of the most important agencies for plant conservation is the Forest Research Institute of Malaysia, commonly known as FRIM. This organization plays a key role in the conservation of dipterocarp trees, which provide the mainstay of the southeast Asian timber industry. Located in Kepong, ten miles northwest of Kuala Lumpur, FRIM's grounds cover 600 hectares of experimental planting areas, an arboretum and areas of reafforestation. Visitors are offered tropical forest trails and can also experience the canopy walkway. Work in the herbarium includes important assessments of the conservation status of the threatened dipterocarp species and other plants of Malaysia.

Another important botanic garden in peninsular Malaysia is the Rimba Ilmu, the botanic garden of the University of Malaya. This garden, which was officially opened in 1974, was developed on a hilly site of about 40 hectares on an abandoned rubber estate. The main aim of the garden has always been to study and conserve the immense diversity of the tropical rainforest flora, and, in doing so, to foster in students and the wider public an increased awareness of the natural environment.

Rimba Ilmu translates as 'Forest of Knowledge' in the Malay language. The garden has been developed to have the feel of a rainforest and concentrates on growing native Malaysian plants.

Tropical ferns and palms at Rimba Ilmu botanic garden.

Photo: BGCI

# THAILAND: A MAGNIFICENT ROYAL GARDEN

Photo: Mr Somkaul Suk-ieam/Queen Sirikit Botanic Garden

In Thailand, the Queen Sirikit Botanic Garden is a magnificent garden close to the city of Chiang Mai in the north of the country. Established in the lush mountains of Doi Pui-Suthep, the garden enjoys a stunning natural setting and covers an area of just over 1,000 hectares.

The indigenous vegetation is dry deciduous forest and one of the natural features of the botanic garden is a spectacular waterfall. Officially opened in 1996, the garden was designed from the outset as a Thai plant conservation centre, where botanical research and study are undertaken to help maintain the impressive biodiversity of Thailand. Collection and propagation of the Thai flora is undertaken for conservation purposes, with particular attention paid to rare and endangered species, and to economically valuable species such as native orchids, medicinal plants, and sustainable wood resources.

The flora of Thailand is remarkably rich, with almost as many plant species as the whole of Europe. Many of these are not yet documented or studied, and so the new research facilities provided by Queen Sirikit will greatly enhance the capacity for understanding Thailand's unique biodiversity.

RIGHT ABOVE: Orchids such as this *Dendrobium* grow in the native dipterocarp forests at the Queen Sirikit Botanic Garden. In the past, trade in wild Thai orchids was a major threat but now the country is a leading supplier of cultivated orchids.

RIGHT: The magnificent glasshouse of the garden replicates the traditional botanic garden image within a tropical setting.

Photo: Mr Somkaul Suk-ieam/Queen Sirikit Botanic Garden

LEFT: A native species of *Afgekia* with horticultural potential, growing in Queen Sirikit Botanic Garden.

LEFT BELOW: Ornamental plantings are interspersed with remnants of natural forest within the garden.

Photo: BGCI

Photo: Mr Somkaul Suk-ieam/Queen Sirikit Botanic Garden

Photo: Kemal Jufri

# INDONESIA: ORCHIDS, FERNS AND MOSSES

One of the most celebrated of Asia's botanic gardens is the Kebun Raya at Bogor, on the Indonesian island of Java. About 30 miles from the sprawling, densely populated capital of Jakarta, the Bogor Botanic Garden is situated on the slope of Mount Salak. Bogor has cooler weather than Jakarta and in 1744 the Dutch Governor-General, Baron Gustaaf von Imhoff, chose it as the site to build a summer-house, called Buitenzorg. For two centuries the Dutch rulers remained in residence at this site, replacing the summer-house with a more imposing palace. For a brief period the British occupied Java, and during their stay the botanic garden was created next to Buitenzorg and officially opened to the public in 1817. The Dutch nurtured the garden on their return, and it became an important research centre for tropical crops such as cassava, tea, oil palm and cinchona. The garden was also developed as a fine landscaped park for the enjoyment of the colonial elite.

Nowadays the Bogor Botanic Garden has an important role to play in plant conservation, education and taxonomic research. The garden itself has over 15,000 plant species, including extensive orchid collections. Part of the garden is conserved as original rainforest.

Above Bogor, in an area of cooler climate and heavy rainfall, is the botanic garden of Cibodas, considered by many to be one of the most beautiful botanic gardens in the world. Cibodas is situated at an altitude of nearly 1,500m on the slopes of Mount Gede-Pangrango and is able to grow many temperate species. The garden covers an area of 125 hectares, about a third of which remains forested. Spectacular ferns are a particular feature of the cool lush gardens, and Cibodas is successfully propagating threatened tree ferns for restoration into the wild.

OPPOSITE: Set amid dramatic scenery, Cibodas Botanic Garden is close to one of Indonesia's most significant national parks, Mt. Gede-Pangrango NP. Linked to Bogo Botanic Garden since 1826, Cibodas is a centre for research into tropical rainforests.

BELOW: Trees covered with epiphytic plants in Cibodas Botanic Garden.

Photo: Kemal Jufri

Propagating ferns at Cibodas Botanic Garden. Tree ferns are collected locally from the wild for sale to visitors, and the garden staff are working with local communities to develop nurseries for the production of ornamental plants.

A unique new conservation feature, the recently opened Cibodas bryophyte park, is believed to be the only outdoor moss park in the world. 250 of Indonesia's 3,000 different species are found in the Cibodas Botanical Garden. Frequently overlooked in conservation planning, the bryophyte garden at Cibodas will help to focus attention on these lowly but attractive and ecologically important plants.

# INDIA: FROM MUGHALS TO MODERN TECHNOLOGY

India has a rich heritage of gardens, ranging from the pleasure grounds of the Mughal Emperors to modern scientific research centres. The Mughal gardens were heavily influenced by traditional Arabic garden design, which spread throughout the Islamic world. A classic feature of Islamic gardens is its division into four equal parts, separated by water channels in the shape of a cross, reflecting the four divisions of the primordial paradise, and the Mughal gardens of India stuck faithfully to this plan. The ornamental gardens laid out before colonial times include Ram Bagh, in Agra, which was developed by the Emperor Babur following his invasion of northern India in 1526, and represents the earliest forms of Mughal garden. Typically, the gardens were laid out on three levels, one where the emperor would give his public audiences and one reserved for the harem.

The garden of Shalamar, "the abode of love", in Srinagar was created in 1629 on the northwest bank of Lake Dal. Other gardens of the area with equally poetic names incorporated features such as pools to reflect the mountain peaks, and the most grandiose, the Nashim-Bagh or "garden of breezes", has a series of planted terraces overlooking the lake, linked by impressive staircases.

There are more than 120 botanic gardens in India. Modern botanical studies in India started with the arrival of the British, who, as well as creating the the Royal Botanic Garden, Calcutta, 1787, established botanical gardens at Sibpur, Poona, Saharanpur and Madras under the local governments. The main purpose of these was to cultivate plants of commercial interest, but they also served as general sources of botanical information. Over time it was considered necessary to coordinate the work of the different botanical centres. The Botanical Survey of India was formally created in 1890, with Sir George King, also superintendent of Royal Botanic Garden, Calcutta, as its first director, and it was re-established in 1955, with regional centres at Coimbatore, Pune, Shillong and Dehra Dun. The current aims of the Botanical Survey are to survey and explore India's plant resources, to publish a national flora, and to catalogue endangered species.

The Botanic Garden at Lucknow dates from 1953, on the site of a garden previously known as Sikander Bagh, which is believed to have been laid out in 1800. The botanic garden has played a major role in exploring and utilising economic plant resources. Many of the garden's

activities now relate to rural India, with research focused on developing and applying new knowledge and technologies for the benefit of farmers; promoting access to medicinal plants for primary healthcare; and developing flower preservation techniques for handicrafts.

The area around Shillong is popularly known as the Scotland of the East, because of its beautiful hill setting, its scenery and pleasant climate. The National Orchidarium and Botanic Garden, Shillong, was established in 1959. This is a small garden, planted with native plants to resemble the forests of the Karsi hills, with, at its centre, a small orchid house containing many orchids, some rare and endangered. Also in Shillong is the Barapani Experimental Garden, established in 1966 for the purpose of collecting rare and endangered species of northeast India for cultivation and preservation.

The Noida Botanic Garden in India has the promotion of nature conservation as its main objective. Conservation biology and micro-propagation are two of its research units.

# SRI LANKA: TEA, SPICES AND MEDICINES

The Royal Botanic Gardens in Peradeniya, Sri Lanka, cover an area of 61 hectares on a horse-shoe shaped peninsula, around which flows the Mahaweli, Sri Lanka's longest river. The history of the Royal Botanic Gardens goes as far back as 1371, when King Wickramabahu III came to the throne and kept court at Peradeniya. The botanic gardens were formed in 1821, six years after the final conquest of the Kandyan Kingdom. A Dutch-style building was constructed in the precincts of the Buddhist temple, to serve as the director's quarters, and this building now houses the National Herbarium and a seed bank. Among the fine historic trees growing in the botanic garden are a Cannonball Tree, *Couroupita guianensis*, planted by King George V and Queen Mary in 1901, a Tamarind, *Tamarandus indica*, planted by the Rt Hon D. S. Senanayake, the first prime minister of Sri Lanka, to commemorate Independence Day on 4 February 1948, and a specimen of *Bauhinia variegata* (known as the Mountain Ebony or Orchid Tree), planted in 1967 by Mrs Indira Gandhi, then prime minister of India.

As with other colonial gardens, the Royal Botanic Gardens, Peradeniya, worked on the introduction and acclimatization of useful plants, such as tea, rubber, cocoa, cinchona, vanilla, fruits, and trees for shade and timber. The garden also helped to improve varieties of species like clove and nutmeg. Now the functions of the garden include conservation, with a focus on orchids and the study of medicinal plants. Over 300 species used in indigenous and Ayurvedic medicine systems are in cultivation at the garden.

Other botanic gardens in Sri Lanka include those at Hakgala, established by Dr G. H. K. Thwaites in 1861, for the experimental introduction of cinchona to the island. The site was once the pleasure garden of Ravana, of the Ramayana epic, and is thought to have been one of the places where the beautiful Sita (consort of Rama, King of Ayodya in India) was hidden by the demon king. The Gampaha (Henarathgoda) Botanic Garden was also established by Thwaites. He began this garden in 1876 for the introduction of rubber. The original consignment of 1,919 seedlings of rubber, sent through Kew Gardens and raised from seeds obtained by Sir Henry Wickham from Brazil, were propagated and planted here.

One of the oldest gardens in Asia, the Royal Botanic Gardens at Peradeniya have played an important role in the study of useful plants.

The Popham Arboretum in the centre of Sri Lanka was established in 1963 on three hectares in the dry heartland of the Island. Mr "Sam" Popham was a retired English tea planter who lived a hermit-like life in a cottage near Kandalama. He attempted to regenerate old dry-zone forest that had been degraded by agriculture, his main method being to encourage natural seedling regeneration rather than using nursery techniques.

About 70 hardwood species were established. In 1978 a cyclone destroyed many of the plantations in the island, but the native trees in this area were left intact. In 1989 Popham returned to England and gifted the arboretum to the Institute of Fundamental Studies (IFS)

in Kandy, stipulating that the indigenous forest should be maintained and no exotics introduced. It is now managed by the tree society of Sri Lanka (Ruk Rakaganno).

Botanic gardens throughout Asia vary greatly in terms of size, style and heritage. Working together they represent an impressive force for science and conservation. This will become even more important as the pace of development continues to increase, bringing with it further deforestation and urbanization. The well-established gardens are helping with the development of new botanic gardens, in countries such as Cambodia and Laos, providing conservation resource centres for the future.

Although noted for its fine collection of trees and flowering shrubs, the garden at Peradeniya also has beds dedicated to the cultivation of annuals and perennials.

# Chapter 6

## AUSTRALASIA

The natural heritage of Australasia includes
a stunning flora, with around 80 per cent of the
native species endemic to the region. The scientific
description of these unique plants began in the late
eighteenth century with the arrival of European
colonists, and today many of the species they
named are grown around the world.

The scientific description of Australia's unique plants began with the work of Joseph Banks, who joined Cook on his first journey to the South Pacific in 1768–71. The primary objective of this historic voyage was to record the transit of Venus across the sun, but of more interest to Banks was the recording of the fauna and flora of the new lands. Banks helped to finance Cook's expedition of discovery, providing around £10,000 towards the costs, and was also a correspondent of Linnaeus, who suggested that the newly discovered country of Australia should be named 'Banksia'. Although this did not happen, a uniquely Australian plant genus is now known by this name. Meanwhile, the region's botanic gardens continue to serve as centres of research and display of some of the most extraordinary flora found anywhere in the world.

# AUSTRALIA: SAND AND SPINIFEX

Australia's vast, arid interior covers 90 per cent of the country. In such conditions creating a garden is not easy, but the Alice Springs Desert Park works with, rather than against, the elements. The Desert Park has a different concept from the traditional botanic garden or zoo, combining elements of both to form a 'biopark', which portrays the ecosystems of central Australia and shows how the local native Australians relate to biodiversity. The desert Aborigines have an intimate knowledge of the land on which they are dependent and have developed extraordinary survival strategies. The early European settlers had no comprehension of the rich social and spiritual life of the original people of Australia and generally treated them with callous disregard at best. In Aboriginal life, the acquisition of material wealth is generally held to be less important than having a rich religious and social life, many of their religious practices being related to the need to secure plants and animals for food.

Women have traditionally been involved in the collection of wild plants and thus exerted considerable power through their role as providers of daily nutritional needs. Over 140 different wild plant species continue to provide food in the arid interior of Australia, in the form of tubers, fruits and seeds. *Acacia* seeds, for example, are eaten and, along with grass seeds, form an important component of the Aboriginal diet. Fresh pods are collected from the trees and roasted to separate the seed and destroy the bitter juices. More generally, dry pods are collected and the seeds released by a process known as 'yandying'. In this process a long wooden dish is used to separate the edible parts of the plant, such as the seeds of *Acacia*, from the bitter-tasting pods.

Against a backdrop of the MacDonnell Ranges, the Alice Springs Desert Park contains various habitats that have been created in a core area of 52 hectares. Enclosures of birds, reptiles and mammals are displayed against the desert vegetation. All the plant species in the Desert Park are native to central Australia. The Sand Country habitat contains red dunes, in which some species have germinated naturally from seed within the imported sand. They grow alongside planted spiky perennial spinifex grasses *Triodia* spp., so characteristic of Australian deserts. The woodland habitat has plants such as Mulga, *Acacia aneura*, Thozet's Box, *Eucalyptus thozetiana*, and the Fruit Salad Bush, *Pterocaulon sphacelatum*. An enclosure of Red Kangaroo and Emu can be seen in this woodland setting.

Alice Springs Desert Park provides a fascinating

introduction to the desert ecosystems of Australia. It is located near the MacDonnell Ranges National Park, which protects rare plants and animals in the harsh natural landscape that has been home to the Aborigines for millennia. In total Australia has over 100 botanic gardens, and collectively these have a strong commitment to the conservation of Australia's unique flora. The country has a wide range of vegetation types which include magnificent tropical and temperate rainforests along with the diverse drylands, and over 20,000 native flowering plant species. Sadly, more than 60 Australian plant species are now thought to be extinct in the wild, and over 1,180 are considered to be threatened. Since the beginning of European settlement there have been major changes in the way native vegetation is managed for agriculture, with altered fire and grazing patterns which have impacted on the native flora. Forest clearance, and the introduction of weeds, feral animals and diseases have also affected the survival of many plant species. Most of the gardens are in lusher environments than the harsh conditions of Alice Springs, and they are able to grow a wide array of interesting plant species.

## TREE FERNS AND LEATHERWOOD

The Australian National Botanic Gardens in Canberra has created a rainforest environment within the grounds of the garden. The Rainforest Gully was originally a dry area with *Eucalyptus* trees, but now has humid vegetation typical of east coast Australian rainforests. Strolling along the walkway gives visitors a sense of being deep in the lush forest. Tasmanian rainforest plants are planted in the lowest part of the gully, with tree ferns, *Dicksonia antarctica*, growing under mature trees of the Blackwood, *Acacia melanoxylon*. The gully also contains examples of trees unique to Tasmania, such as the Leatherwood, *Eucryphia lucida*, and the Huon Pine, *Lagarostrobos franklinii*, a valuable source of timber but now under

Photo: BGCI

RIGHT: Tree ferns at the Australian National Botanic Gardens in Canberra.

BELOW: An interpretative sign for Sturt's Desert Pea, *Swainsona formosa*, at the Australian Arid Lands Botanic Garden at Port Augusta.

threat in the wild. Towards the upper end of the gully are montane species typical of the rainforests in the far north of Queensland.

## RESEARCH AND INTERPRETATION

The plants of the Australian National Botanic Gardens are important for research as well as for display and education. The living collections of the gardens comprise almost one-third of the Australian flora. The

Centre for Plant Biodiversity Research, which is associated with the Australian National Botanic Gardens, undertakes scientific research on biodiversity as a basis for conservation, management and sustainable use of the Australian flora. It provides a national focus for botanical data, drawing on the Australian National Herbarium, which houses a collection of 1.3 million plant specimens, dating back to Captain Cook's 1770 expedition. Taxonomic research on native plants remains important, as new species are still being described in Australia, and documentation of the geographical distribution and ecological relationships of species is important for conservation planning. The maintenance and recovery of rare and threatened species is a significant element of the Centre's work. The Centre drew on its extensive resources, and those of Environment Australia, to produce the fourth edition of *Rare or Threatened Australian Plants,* published in 1996. Conservation biology relates not only to rare species, but to an understanding of the ecology and the dynamics of larger ecosystems. Research on the effects on the Australian environment of fire, disease and fragmentation is vital in the development of strategies for integrated land use and revegetation projects.

## AUSTRALIA'S OLDEST BOTANIC GARDEN

The Royal Botanic Gardens, Sydney, is Australia's oldest botanic garden and the country's oldest scientific institution. Established in 1816 by Governor Macquarie, it became a "Royal" garden in 1959. The parkland surrounding the Botanic Gardens is still known as the Sydney Domain. The land, containing the site of the first farm in Australia, was originally set aside in 1788 by Governor Phillip as his private reserve. It covered the area east of the Tank Stream to the head of Walla Mulla Bay. The farm on this land was established for growing grain, but was soon moved because of the poor sandy soil of the area. The collection and study of plants at the Botanic Gardens in Sydney began with the appointment of the first Colonial Botanist, Charles Fraser, in 1817. Expanded and reorganized, the gardens were opened to the general public in 1831. Over the years the gardens grew as the land of the Domain was developed, but the parkland remained an important buffer.

The first director of the botanic garden in Sydney was John Carne Bidwell, appointed in 1847. The tree species *Araucaria bidwellii*, a relative of the Monkey Puzzle, is named after him. The following year Charles Moore took over and remained as director until 1896. Charles Moore did much to develop the botanic gardens in their modern form, reclaiming land behind the Farm Cove seawall, thus adding significantly to the area of the Royal Botanic Gardens. In 1862 Sydney's first zoo was opened within the botanic gardens, remaining there until 1883, when most of it was transferred to Moore Park. During these years much of the remnant natural vegetation of the surrounding Domain was removed and planted as parkland. The Moreton Bay Figs, one of the major elements of this planting, continue to dominate the landscape.

Modern features of the gardens include a rose garden, fernery, herb garden, oriental garden and conservatories. A rare and threatened species garden was established in 1998, and a garden has recently been developed to link with the Aboriginal people of Sydney; a display shows the woodland vegetation that would have existed around Sydney Harbour prior to European settlement two centuries ago.

## THE WOLLEMI PINE

The Royal Botanic Gardens at Sydney also has satellite gardens, the Mount Tomah Botanic Garden and Mount Annan Botanic Garden. Research at Mount Annan Botanic Garden is largely concerned with the conservation and horticulture of Australian plants, including strategies for reproduction in the wild and in cultivation, cultivation requirements and seed storage. Without doubt the most famous species currently being studied is the remarkable *Wollemia nobilis*, or Wollemi Pine. Botanists were astonished by the discovery of this species in 1994. A member of the Araucariaceae family, it represents the last of an evolutionary line of conifers

The Royal Botanic Gardens in Sydney enjoy a superb natural location.

Photo: Tony Kirkham

The Wollemi Pine has become a cause célèbre in plant conservation. Following its discovery at a secret location close to Sydney in 1994, the plant has been propagated and distributed to selected botanic gardens around the world. This specimen is at the Royal Botanic Gardens, Kew.

that was thought to be extinct for millions of years. In September 1994, David Noble, an officer with the New South Wales National Parks and Wildlife Service, discovered striking, tall trees of a type he was not familiar with. The trees were growing in a deep, narrow canyon in a rugged area now designated as the Wollemi National Park and situated only 93 miles from Sydney. This is the largest wilderness area in New South Wales and forms part of the recently declared Greater Blue Mountains World Heritage Area – a maze of canyons, cliffs and undisturbed forest. Based on this discovery a new genus was described, *Wollemia*, with this single species. The closest relatives of the Wollemi Pine are trees of the *Araucaria* genus, which includes Bidwell's Pine, the Monkey Puzzle Tree and Parana Pine, and the related genus *Agathis*.

In the wild, most of the adult Wollemi Pine trees, and a number of seedlings and juvenile plants, have been tagged and measured for height and trunk diameter. This provides a basis for long-term monitoring of survival and growth rates, which can then be related to the history of trees using tree-ring and growth analyses. Less than a hundred plants are known in the wild population. The species is now relatively well established in cultivation, in conservation collections around the world. The individuals both in the wild and in cultivation are carefully guarded to ensure their survival. The Wollemi Pine has become a flagship species for plant conservation, highlighting the need for both protection of the natural habitat and ex-situ conservation measures as an insurance policy.

## A STRONG COMMITMENT TO CONSERVATION

The Adelaide Botanic Garden is another fine Australian Botanic Garden with historic significance, excellent plant collections and a strong commitment to conservation. The early history of the Adelaide Botanic Garden was, however, fraught with difficulty. A botanic garden was established in 1837, only one year after South Australia was proclaimed. The garden was included in Colonel Light's plan for the city but unfortunately the area set aside was an island in the River Torrens, which regularly flooded. This garden site was soon abandoned, and the second site was also unsuccessful because of invading stock from the adjacent parklands. The third site selected was more suitable, situated on the north bank of the river, and development of the garden began in 1839, but financial difficulties resulted in its closure soon after it opened. In 1854 the Agricultural and Horticultural Society recommended the establishment of a new 18.5-hectare garden on its present site. George Francis was appointed superintendent in 1855, and in 1857 it opened to the public. In 1894 the associated Botanic Park was dedicated on land that had been used for grazing police horses.

Francis's planting is said to have been influenced by the gardens at Kew and Versailles, together with Dutch and German influences, and the garden and some of its buildings still retain a Northern European flavour. Many old tree plantings survive, such as the Moreton's Bay Fig Avenue, planted in 1866. In 1868 the massive Victoria Water-lily, discovered in South America by the brother of Adelaide Botanic Garden's then director, Dr Richard Schomburgk, flowered in the Victoria House and was of huge public interest. Since then its cultivation and flowering has been a feature of Adelaide Botanic Garden.

The Palm House (now called the Tropical House) was imported from Germany and opened in 1877. It is nationally recognized as an important historic building and is listed on the National Estate. In its early days the garden was important for agricultural plant acclimatization, with varieties of wheat, oats and sorghum introduced here, and various fruit and vines were tested.

Adelaide Botanic Garden has two associated gardens, the Mount Lofty Botanic Garden, comprising 100 hectares in the Mount Lofty Ranges, and Wittunga Botanic Garden, covering 15.4 hectares. Established in 1902 as a private formal English garden, the Wittunga garden was given to the State in 1965. By that time it was growing a wide range of Australian and South African plants. The network of three gardens at different altitudes allows a wide range of plants to be grown from arctic alpines at the Mount Lofty Botanic Garden to sub-tropicals and tropicals at Adelaide.

## A NATURAL SANCTUARY FOR WILDLIFE

The Royal Botanic Gardens Melbourne was established in 1846 at a site on the southern bank of the Yarra River. In 1857, the Gardens' first full-time director, Ferdinand von Mueller, was appointed. Mueller was one of the most acclaimed botanists of the 19th century, travelling extensively in Australia, collecting and classifying both the flora and fauna and introducing Australian plants to botanic gardens and herbaria around the world. In 1855,

The Bicentennial Conservatory at Adelaide Botanic Garden is the largest single-span conservatory in the southern hemisphere. It is 100m in length and houses lowland tropical rainforest plants.

Photo: Botanic Gardens of Adelaide

*Kingia australis* is a slow-growing plant confined to the south of Western Australia. It is also in cultivation in a number of botanic gardens.

he was appointed botanist of the North West Australia Expedition and, on a journey of over 5,000 miles, he collected nearly 2,000 species of plants. In 1873 Mueller was succeeded by William Guilfoyle, who created the Gardens' "picturesque" landscape style with extensive lawns, lakes and meandering paths. The classic garden design worked well in the temperate climate of Melbourne, which allows a wide range of both temperate and tropical species to be grown successfully.

Today, the Royal Botanic Gardens Melbourne has more than 51,000 individual plants in cultivation, representing over 12,000 different species. As well as being a natural sanctuary for native wildlife, including Black Swans, Bell-birds, Cockatoos and Kookaburras, the gardens are committed to the conservation of native plants of Victoria. Out of the approximately 3,200 native species of the State, nearly 700 are considered to be threatened with extinction. The botanic gardens are collaborating with the Millennium Seedbank at Kew to preserve the seed of endangered endemics, and are also carrying out very important research to assess the impact of climate change on the native flora and on the spread of weeds and plant diseases.

## BUSHLAND ENHANCED WITH RICH LOCAL FLORA

Western Australia has a rich flora, with many endemic plant species. Kings Park and Botanic Garden in West Perth displays many of the elements of this floral

Photo: Bert Van den Wollenberg

diversity and has become a popular tourist destination. Before European settlement, the land occupied by the botanic garden was an important ceremonial and spiritual dreaming place for people of the Whadjug tribe of the Nyoongar nation. The Swan River colony was settled in 1829 and, two years later, the first Surveyor General, Septimus Rose, set aside Mount Eliza and its surrounding land for public use. In 1872, after much timber had been cut, 175 hectares were declared a reserve, known as Perth Park. In 1895 Sir John Forrest, the first premier of Western Australia, began to develop the park and was instrumental in changing its name to the Kings Park to mark the accession to the throne of King Edward VII in 1901.

The original concept was for an English-style park with avenues of shady trees. Some of the introduced trees, such as English oaks, did not thrive. The climate and strongly drained soils made Kings Park difficult terrain to plant, and much remained bushland. Natural bushland remains in the botanic garden today, enhanced with plantings of the rich local flora. There has been an increased focus on restoration of the bushland in recent years.

In 1959 a State Botanic Garden was established in Kings Park, complementing the botanic gardens in other Australian States which had been developed in the colonial period. Work began to develop the garden in 1962. From the outset there was a commitment to cultivating the native flora of the southwest of the State, which has a rate of endemism of about 70 per cent. Another specialism was the cultivation of plants from other regions of the world which share a Mediterranean climate. The Biodiversity Conservation Centre at KPBG was opened in 2005.

The extensive nursery and experimental section at King's Park has researched the cultivation of many native plants, in particular the halophytes, or salt-loving plants, some of which have economic importance for the pastoral rangelands. King's Park also has a major commitment to the restoration of degraded natural habitats using indigenous plant species, working in partnership with the mining industry which is thriving in Western Australia, fuelled by the rapid growth of the Chinese economy. Western Australia is one of the world's leading areas for the production of iron ore, with mines falling within a global biodiversity hotspot.

## WORKING WITH THE MINING INDUSTRY

Ecologists and conservationists around the world are working to match the pace of landscape alterations with restoration of the ecosystem. Botanic gardens are well placed to assist in these efforts because of their specialized knowledge of natural plant diversity and cultivation techniques. The impact of the mining sector on landscape-level changes and the loss of some species is highly significant in Western Australia. King's Park first developed a partnership with the mineral sands (titanium) extraction industry in 1984, when the company was attempting to restore a rare species, Hidden Beard Heath, *Leucopogon obtectus*, Ericaceae, threatened by the mining operation. The research programme, carried out over a decade, resulted in an improved understanding of the genetic diversity, seed biology, mycorrhiza and the role of fire in the recruitment of the rare species. Significantly, the programme also developed into larger research programmes involving restoration ecology of Ericaceae across many other companies in the mining industry in Australia. Lasting benefits of the programme include improved methods for topsoil handling to optimize mycorrhiza and species recovery. With mining industry support, King's Park scientists have been able to establish conservation techniques and management for rare and threatened species in non-mining situations. The restoration of orchid populations and the restoration and management of urban bushland areas have been particular success stories.

## BOTANICAL HERITAGE

The original botanic gardens established in Darwin were created to trial food crops. The gardens were begun on their present site in June 1886. By then, the town of Darwin was 16 years old and the establishment of these gardens was the third formal attempt to select a site which would be suitable for experimenting with plants of economic importance. The level area where the gardens are today was once very swampy. Today much of the original vegetation has disappeared, but there are remnant representatives still to be seen; the Mangrove community has increased as a result of drainage development. Now the Darwin Botanical Gardens, renamed the George Brown Darwin Botanical Garden in honour of a recent Mayor, are a good place to see

Photo: George Brown/Darwin Botanical Garden

The Fountain Pond is beautifully set within the George Brown Darwin Botanical Garden.

tropical plants and the Aboriginal botanical heritage.

The Royal Tasmanian Botanic Gardens are the second oldest botanic gardens in Australia, established two years after the Royal Botanic Gardens, Sydney. Originally the acclimatization of food plants was one of the main functions of the gardens, but now one of the special features is the Tasmanian Plants display, celebrating the island's flora, with over 600 species. Another unusual display is the Subantarctic Plant House, showing plants from Macquarie Island, in the Southern Ocean, lying 930 miles southeast of Tasmania, roughly halfway between Australia and Antarctica. The island is managed by Australia as a protected area of

global significance for its marine mammal and seabird populations. The natural vegetation consists of tussock grassland, with *Poa foliosa*, *P. cookii* and *Stilbocarpus polaris*; Macquarie Island Cabbage, which was eaten by whalers to prevent scurvy; feldmark, which covers approximately half the island with the cushion-forming *Azorella macquariensis*; and areas of mire vegetation. These plants can be seen in the Subantarctic Plant House, displayed against a background of painted landscapes. Lighting, temperature and humidity are carefully controlled to represent the subantarctic conditions of Macquarie Island.

# NEW ZEALAND

New Zealand has 20 botanic gardens. The first was established in June 1863, on what is now the site of the Registry of the University of Otago, in Dunedin, South Island. After a severe flood from the Water of Leith, it was transferred to the present 32-hectare site in 1886. The Dunedin Botanic Garden contains many specimen trees over 100 years old, including the "Royal" Oak planted in 1863 to commemorate the marriage of King Edward VII and Princess Alexandra.

The Wellington Botanic Garden was established soon after, in 1869, on a 5-hectare site called the Colonial Botanic Garden, under the control of a New Zealand Institute. Additional land was added, and since 1891 it has been controlled by Wellington City Council. Trees growing today on Druid Hill and Magpie Spur grew from seedlings planted at that time, and are some of the oldest exotic trees in New Zealand. Provision was made for the government to use 2.4 hectares on the Kelburn ridge as the site for the observatory – this is now New Zealand's national observatory. The early structures and design of the garden, with a Victorian fountain and magnificent wrought iron gate, give Wellington Botanic Garden the air of a colonial Victorian Garden. It is classified as a Garden of National Significance by the Royal New Zealand Institute of Horticulture and is an Historic Places Trust Heritage Area. More recent features of the garden include one of the best rose gardens in New Zealand, with more than a hundred types of rose, and works of art by Henry Moore, Andrew Drummond and Chris Booth. There is a Peace Garden, with a flame based on that created by the atomic bomb dropped on Hiroshima in 1945. The flame was presented by the people of Japan to New Zealand as a tribute to efforts to halt the spread of atomic weapons.

The Christchurch Botanic Gardens date back to 1863, when an English oak was planted to commemorate the marriage of Queen Victoria's eldest son, Prince Albert Edward, to Princess Alexandra of Denmark. The grounds of the Botanic Gardens

Dunedin Botanic Garden has been in its current location for over a century and contains many impressive mature trees.

The Auckland Regional Botanic Gardens display threatened native plants from northern New Zealand in a specially designed conservation garden.

Photo: Peter Thompson

encompass an area of 30 hectares, the majority of this being within a loop of the Avon River. Until 1863, the gardens were largely natural wetlands and sand dunes. There are many large trees, several of which are more than 120 years old, which form a majestic background to the numerous plant collections and sweeping lawns.

## TEMPERATE AND SUB-TROPICAL RAINFOREST

The Auckland Regional Botanic Gardens have been developed on former farmland at a site purchased in 1967. The wide range of soil and climate conditions it contained was representative of those found across the Auckland region, making it suitable for trialling plants for suitability for home gardening. In 1973 a plant nursery was developed and planting began the following year, the gardens opening to the public in 1982. The gardens include formal gardens, roses, herbs, conifers and rock gardens and two ornamental lakes. There is a large collection of native plants, including New Zealand's largest collection of flaxes of traditional Maori weaving cultivars (46 varieties), 90 varieties of the ornamental genus *Hebe*, and many cultivars of Pohutukawa, *Metrosideros excelsa*. As the Auckland gardens are the most northerly botanic garden in the country, the native plant collection concentrates on plants which occur naturally in northern New Zealand, characterized by dense temperate and sub-tropical rainforest.

Within the Auckland Regional Botanic Gardens, natural forest covers ten hectares and a native plant trail through this allows visitors to see the mixed broadleaf and podocarp forest which originally covered much of the lowland of New Zealand. Species that grow here include the native tree ferns: *Cyathea cunninghamii*, Gulley Fern; *Cyathea dealbata*, Ponga or Silver Fern; *Cyathea medullaris*, Mamaku or Black Tree Fern; *Dicksonia squarrosa*, Wheki; and the gymnosperms: *Agathis australis*, Kauri; *Dacrycarpus dacrydioides*, Kahikatea; *Dacrydium cupressinum*, Rimu; *Phyllocladus trichomanoides*, the Celery Pine; *Podocarpus totara*; Totara; *Prumnopitys ferruginea*, Miro; and *Prumnopitys taxifolia*, Matai.

The Threatened Native Plant Garden (TNPG) at the Auckland Regional Botanic Gardens is a new collection, opened in 2001 as a showcase for plant conservation. The garden is divided into habitat sections representing the different types of forest, and gumland, a term for the previously logged Kauri, *Agathis australis*, forests which have heavily nutrient-leached soils. There are also more restricted and specialized habitats, such as lava field, wetland, sand-dune, shellbank and saltmarsh. Within these habitat sections, typical species have been planted along with examples of threatened species displayed in naturalistic settings. In total, around 170 species of native plants of the Auckland and northland regions of New Zealand, including the offshore islands, are threatened in some way. Plants in the Auckland collection include the Rock Koromiko, *Hebe bishopiana*, a scrambling shrub with mauve flowers, endemic to the west coast where it is threatened by erosion and invasive weeds. Another species in cultivation is the Shore Spurge, *Euphorbia glauca*, which clings precariously to a few cliff habitats in the Auckland area. Matua Kumara 'large petals', *Geranium solanderi*, is one of the endemic plants growing naturally on lava fields. This habitat type is seriously depleted in Auckland and so ex-situ conservation becomes increasingly important for the species that grow only there.

The Three Kings Trumpet Vine, *Tecomanthe speciosa*, is a vigorous climber with large, cream trumpet flowers. It is another of the New Zealand conservation success stories and can be seen in the botanic garden at Auckland. When it was discovered in the wild in 1945, on Great Island (one of the Three Kings Islands), only one individual was found. Fortunately the plant can be propagated from both seed and cuttings and it was therefore possible to establish it in cultivation. The main threats to the flora of the Three Kings Islands in the past were clearance by Maoris, who inhabited Great Island for two centuries or more up to about 1840, and then grazing by goats, introduced to the island in 1889. The goats were removed in 1946 and the Three Kings Islands are now managed as a conservation reserve.

# THE SOUTH PACIFIC

The scattered palm-fringed islands of the Pacific Ocean have fragile floras in need of conservation attention. As in the Indian Ocean, introduced species, agricultural development and tourism have all taken their toll on the endemic plants that have evolved here in relative isolation. The botanic gardens of Hawaii (see pp.118–119) are leading the way with plant rescue, the display of endangered plants and plants important in Polynesian culture. Elsewhere in the region there are relatively few botanic gardens, but those that do exist have great potential to contribute to the conservation of plant diversity.

One such site is the Norfolk Island Botanic Garden, managed under Australian conservation legislation. The garden provides an opportunity to see the unique plants of this island and includes an important patch of remnant rainforest.

The Suva Botanical Gardens on Fiji are of historical importance and house the Fiji Museum. They have great potential to become a display area for Fijian flora, and the avenues of Royal Palms and tree ferns date back nearly a century. Fiji's second botanic garden is at the University of the South Pacific (USP) Laucala Campus in Suva. Sadly, both Fiji's gardens have suffered a period of decline, but there are plans for their revival and for the involvement of the university garden in the conservation of Fiji's unique palm species.

*Photo: Ian Rolls*

*Pritchardia pacifica*, the Fiji Fan Palm, is not known in the wild but is a common ornamental species worldwide.

# Chapter 7

# NORTH AMERICA

The native flora of North America is huge and
diverse, reflecting the local variation in ecosystems
and vegetation types. This rich plant heritage is displayed
at more than 350 botanic gardens across the continent,
alongside magnificent glasshouse collections of exotic plants.
The commitment by botanic gardens to the study and
conservation of the North American flora is impressive,
and these skills and expertise are increasingly
shared with botanic gardens around the world.

The North American botanic gardens represent a strong force for conservation. They are helping to protect and restore native species and natural habitats from the Arctic to the southwestern deserts, and from the prairies to the island peaksof Hawaii. The gardens build on a rich tradition of native plant exploration, scientific discovery and links with European gardens going back over 150 years.

# GARDENS ACROSS THE UNITED STATES

The oldest botanic gardens of the USA include Missouri Botanical Garden in St Louis and the New York Botanic Garden. The development of both these gardens was heavily influenced by the European garden tradition and the involvement of the Royal Botanic Gardens, Kew. Missouri Botanical Garden was established by Henry Shaw, an Englishman who was born in Sheffield in 1800. Shaw was educated at Mill Hill School, in Middlesex, which had a fine garden with exotic plants, including three Cedars of Lebanon said to have been planted by Linnaeus. In 1819, Henry Shaw sailed to Canada with his father, Joseph Shaw, in search of new fortunes. Henry settled in St Louis in the same year and soon prospered in the hardware and cutlery business. At the same time he retained his love of gardening, which had developed during his school years.

With his increasing wealth, Henry travelled extensively in Europe and was inspired to create a public garden close to his country home, Tower Grove, a short distance from downtown St Louis. In 1856, Henry Shaw wrote to William Hooker, the first official Director of Kew and father of Joseph Hooker, who followed him in this role, asking for "hints and information" to establish a public botanic garden. Hooker put Shaw in touch with Asa Gray at Harvard University and George Engelmann at the St Louis Academy of Science. Engelmann was a German-born physician and botanist who had a particular interest in cacti and conifers. He became Shaw's scientific adviser, and persuaded him to include a herbarium and library within the botanic garden.

## SHAW'S GARDEN

Missouri Botanical Garden is still known by residents of St Louis as Shaw's Garden. Today it is a world leader in botanical research and plant conservation, as well as a much-loved public garden. The garden works collaboratively with experts in over 30 countries and each year scientists from MBG describe around 200 new plant species. The research and documentation of plant species in China, Vietnam, Madagascar and Latin America contribute directly to their conservation and the conservation of the habitats where they grow. Missouri Botanical Garden is also very actively involved in the conservation of threatened plants within the US.

Stern's Medlar, *Mespilus canescens*, is one of the endangered plant species that MBG is helping to save. A member of the rose family, this tree grows only in an isolated pocket of the USA and its only close relative is the common cultivated Medlar, a native of southeast Europe and west Asia. Incredibly, Stern's Medlar was not discovered until 1990, and the only known wild trees are in the Mississippi Delta region of Arkansas, where a tiny population clings on. Most of the woodlands in the area have been cleared for agriculture, but fortunately a private landowner has taken steps to ensure that Stern's Medlar is protected through an agreement with the Arkansas Natural Heritage Commission. The trees are carefully monitored to ensure that they are not damaged by local agricultural activities. The long-term chances of survival are being enhanced by research into methods of propagation for the species, which may lead to the re-establishment of wild populations.

Within Missouri Botanical Garden, one of the most celebrated features is the Climatron conservatory. Built in 1960, this was the first geodesic dome to be used as a greenhouse. It now contains around 2,800 tropical plants, displayed in a lowland rainforest setting. Other glasshouses at Missouri include the Shoenberg Temperate House, which features plants from the Mediterranean and has a Moorish garden as its centrepiece, and the Linnaean House, which was built in 1882 and holds Missouri's collection of camellias. The grounds include 23 different display gardens with a variety of statues, sculptures and water features. Within these gardens examples of threatened and endangered native US plants can be seen. In the Dry Streambed Garden, for example, endangered species which form part of the CPC collection are grown alongside the hardy waterlily pond and a variety of ornamental grasses and shrubs.

PAGE 106: US botanic gardens are actively working to save native species such as Royal Catchfly, *Silene regia*.

BELOW: The Climatron conservatory allows tropical rainforest plants to be displayed in St Louis, Missouri.

Photo: J. Monkton

Photo: Robert Benson/NYBG

The Nolen Greenhouses at the New York Botanic Garden were opened in 2005. They maintain permanent living plant collections for research, conservation and ornamental display. A centralized computer network monitors and manages shade, humidity, heat retention, ventilation and temperature.

## A STRONG SCIENTIFIC BASE

The New York Botanic Garden was established in 1896 as a result of campaigning by Nathaniel Lord Britton and his wife Elizabeth. Botany was considered a science particularly suited to women in the 19th century in the USA, and Elizabeth Britton was an acknowledged botanical expert. She travelled with her husband to Kew Gardens in 1888 and on her return gave an illustrated description of Kew to the Torrey Botanical Club. During that same year a Committee was formed to promote and raise funds for the establishment of a botanic garden in Bronx Park. Nathaniel Britton was appointed the first director of the garden when it was established and quickly ensured a strong scientific base for its work.

The New York Botanic Garden is one of the world's finest, with comprehensive science and conservation carried out behind the scenes. One-fifth of the area of the garden is native forest, managed for long-term conservation. Further afield, the botanic garden is actively involved in research to conserve plants in Amazonia, Mexico and Thailand.

New York has another impressive botanic garden based in Brooklyn. Established in 1910, the Brooklyn Botanic Garden was reclaimed from a waste dump and now covers a total of 21 hectares. The garden's chief mission is to educate the public about plants and inform people about ecology and awareness of the environment. This is achieved by means of workshops, training schemes, a range of projects aimed particularly at children, and "safaris" to the Steinhardt Conservatory, This houses plant collections arranged in realistic environments representing a range of global habitats, with arid areas, Mediterranean vegetation and tropical rainforest, and plants from Africa, Asia and the Amazon.

A Children's Garden programme has been in operation at Brooklyn since 1914 (it was the first garden of its kind in the world) and has been much imitated by other institutions. A newer scheme, Project Green Reach, inaugurated in 1989, aims to encourage the study of botany and environmental science in poorer urban communities.

Brooklyn is also taking steps to catalogue and conserve the plant diversity found in the New York metropolitan region, through the 15-year New York Metropolitan Flora Project. Of the endangered species in the USA, more than 266 species native to New York are on the list of endangered plants, and Brooklyn is playing an important part in their conservation.

An institution with research interests further afield is the Arnold Arboretum of Harvard University in Boston,

Massachusetts, whose living collections place particular emphasis on the woody species not only of North America but also of eastern Asia. The living collections are maintained in naturalistic style and are arranged by family and genus, to facilitate study. There are particularly extensive collections of *Fagus* (beech), *Magnolia*, *Quercus* (oak), *Rhododendron* and *Syringa* (lilac).

The Arnold Arboretum has a long history of working with the plants of eastern Asia, and in the early 1900s employed plant collectors such as Ernest H. Wilson, the famous British plant-hunter, to travel on lengthy expeditions in Asia, collecting plants and seeds for study in the West. It was during a search for trees for the Arnold Arboretum in China that Wilson discovered *Lilium regale*, which adorns many gardens today. It is said that, at one point, an estimated 2,000 new species were taken back to Boston by Wilson in a four-month period. Species regarded as too tender for the Massachusetts climate were sent to Scotland, and many of Wilson's rhodendrons and trees can still be seen today at the Royal Botanic Gardens Edinburgh's specialist garden at Dawyck, near Peebles in the Scottish Borders.

Current research projects at the Arnold Arboretum include investigation of the Hengduan Mountain region in China, an area on the southeastern edge of the Tibetan plateau and a biodiversity hotspot. Here an estimated 30–40 per cent of China's 30,000 species can be found, some 3,000 of them endemic. Material is studied in China and in the US. The arboretum is also currently aiming to broaden its holdings of *Acer*, *Carya*, *Fagus*, *Syringa* and *Tsuga* for conservation and evaluation purposes.

## DISPLAY, STUDY AND EXCHANGE

The United States Botanic Garden (USBG) in Washington DC moved to its present location in 1933. Its history goes back as far as 1816, when the idea of creating a botanic garden in the city to collect, grow and distribute plants was first planned. In 1842 the idea was revived after overseas expeditions brought plants from all around the globe back to Washington, and glasshouses were built especially to accommodate them.

Today, the garden features a majestic conservatory set within several hectares of grounds. An adjacent hectare is destined to become a National Garden. The collections include crop plants of economic importance, medicinal plants, orchids, cacti and succulents, cycads,

The Cherry Walk at Brooklyn Botanic Garden is a popular spring attraction. The garden has more than 200 cherry trees, comprising 42 species and varieties. In terms of its size and diversity, this collection is unmatched outside Japan.

Photo: Barbara Alper/Brooklyn Botanic Garden

bromeliads and ferns, and a stock of over 26,000 plants is used for display, study and exchange.

The US Botanic Garden is actively involved in partnerships to save plants. It is, for example, one of 62 botanic gardens, arboreta and other institutions that take part in the Plant Rescue Center Program. As a result of the scheme, hundreds of plants (especially orchids and cacti) have joined the USBG collections. In one example, USBG came to the rescue when an illegal consignment of *Paphiopedilum vietnamense*, a rare Vietnamese orchid, was seized in 1999. The confiscated plants were taken into safekeeping at the garden and a scheme put into operation to safeguard the orchids in future, by making them less rare and vulnerable to unscrupulous collecting through growing seedlings following CITES guidelines. The plants then go on sale at a reasonable price to other botanical gardens and also to the public, reducing the species' rarity and therefore the pressure on wild populations.

## THE APPALACHIAN MOUNTAINS

One of the loveliest natural garden settings in America is home to the North Carolina Arboretum. The southern Appalachian Mountains form a dramatic backdrop to the sprawling 175-hectare Arboretum, which is part of the Bent Creek Experimental Forest, itself part of the Pisgah National Forest. The Arboretum acts as a centre for education, research, conservation and garden demonstration and, besides garden displays, offers visitors wonderful walking and cycling trails through the forest and hills. The Arboretum has been a member of CPC since 1992 and actively participates in conservation of endangered plants, with projects underway to propagate and reintroduce rare Appalachian plants, including rare species of *Crataegus*. Within the French Broad Heartleaf Preserve, the largest known population of *Hexastylis rhombiformis* is protected. The National Native Azalea Repository protects the diversity of deciduous azaleas native to North America.

The mountains form a superb backdrop to the 'Plants of Promise Garden' at the North Carolina Arboreturm.

Photo: Michael Oppenheim/North Carolina Arboretum

Insectivorous *Sarracenia* plants in flower at at the State Botanic Garden, Georgia.

## GEORGIA: SOURCE OF MANY GARDEN FAVOURITES

The flora of the State of Georgia and the southeastern USA is particularly diverse, and drew many European plant hunters from the 17th to the 19th centuries. Tradescant, Clayton, Catesby, Michaux and others came here on field expeditions and sent hundreds of newly discovered species back to Europe. The famous *Franklinia*, named for Benjamin Franklin and now extinct in the wild, was discovered in 1765 by John and William Bartram. The Native Flora Garden within the State Botanic Garden of Georgia, Athens, contains more than 300 different Georgian species, including ferns, trilliums, bloodroot and lady slipper orchids. The International Garden and the Bog Garden also shelter numbers of rare and unusual plants. The International Garden includes a Herb Garden and Physic Garden, illustrating the forerunners of today's botanic gardens, an Age of Exploration section featuring the great plant hunters and an Age of Conservation area, where plants used by American Indians are used to demonstrate how age-old conservation practices were a matter of routine for Indians in the southeastern US.

## RARE TROPICALS IN FLORIDA

The Fairchild Tropical Botanic Garden is a very attractive garden located in Miami. It is one of the world's pre-eminent botanic gardens, with extensive collections of rare tropical plants including palms, cycads, flowering trees and vines. Established in 1938, the 33-hectare garden is one of the region's most popular visitor attractions and offers a variety of programmes in environmental education, conservation and horticulture. An international leader in tropical plant research, Fairchild Tropical Botanic Garden plays an important part in preserving the biodiversity of the tropical environment.

One of the threatened plant species that Fairchild is helping to save is the endangered *Goetzea elegans*, commonly known as Mata Buey or Beautiful Goetzea. This is a small tree with attractive orange-yellow flowers that is found naturally only in the hilly limestone forests of northern Puerto Rico. The wild plants are threatened by hotel construction, other forms of habitat disturbance and destruction and removal of the attractive flowers. Botanists from Fairchild Tropical Botanic Garden are working with local organizations to protect the habitat of

the Beautiful Goetzea and to study propagation and cultivation techniques. Reintroductions from cultivated material can, with careful planning, be used to enhance the remaining wild populations.

## COLORADO'S VARIED ECOSYSTEMS

Denver Botanic Garden in Colorado was one of the first gardens in the USA to emphasize the importance of native plants and promote environmentally responsible horticultural practices, such as water conservation. The main gardens are at a 9-hectare site at York Street in Denver itself, but three additional gardens – Chatfield, the Mount Goliath Alpine Trail and the Centennial Gardens – demonstrate the very varied ecosystems to be found in the State of Colorado. The Botanic Garden has long made its aim "to reverse the degradation and decline of our native flora through conservation, experimentation and the dissemination of knowledge" and, to this end, rare plant populations are carefully studied and monitored. Conservation training programmes are run regularly, in partnership with CPC and the US Botanic Garden in Washington, to train students in conservation techniques. Current subjects of concern include *Astragalus microcymbus* (Skiff Milkvetch), *Gilia caespitosa* (Rabbit Valley Gilia) and *Penstemon harringtonii* (Harrington's Beardtongue). An experimental trial to reintroduce *Eustoma grandiflorum* (Showy Prairie Gentian) is underway at the Rocky Mountain Arsenal National Wildlife Refuge and it is hoped that the population will be self-sustaining.

## THE WEST COAST AND THE DESERT

Huntington Botanical Gardens in Pasadena, California, is said to be one of the most attractive botanic gardens in the world. Huntington House was built between 1906 and 1914 by Henry Edwards Huntington, a leading figure in the development of southern California and a patron of literature and the arts. The house contains a valuable library and a famous collection of English portraits, including *The Blue Boy* by Gainsborough. From the outset, Huntington planned to transform the San Marino Estate he had purchased in 1903 into one of the most

OPPOSITE: The beautiful displays at Fairchild Tropical Botanic Garden are a fitting tribute to the garden's founder, David Fairchild (1869–1954), who travelled the world in search of plants of potential use to the American people.

LEFT: The Japanese Garden at Huntington Botanical Gardens contains a stunning array of interesting plants and architectural features.

Photo: The Huntington Library, Art Collections, and Botanical Gardens ©The Huntington

The Agave Bed at the Desert Botanical Garden, Arizona.

Photo: Adam Rodriguez

California has a very rich native flora and is considered to be one of the world's biodiversity hotspots. With over 6,000 native plants, it has more plant species than any other state in the USA. A large number of the plant species of California are under threat of extinction, with over 200 endemic plants known from fewer than five populations. Botanic gardens such as Rancho Santa Ana Botanic Garden and Santa Barbara Botanic Garden are playing their part to help conserve the rich floral diversity of the State.

Known as California's native garden, Rancho Santa Ana Botanic Garden was created by Susanna Bixby Bryant in 1927 on her ranch in Orange County. The garden was subsequently relocated to Claremont and is now the largest botanical garden dedicated to California's native plants. One critically endangered species in the care of Rancho Santa Ana is the small tree, *Cercocarpus traskiae*, or Catalina Island Mountain Mahogany. Endemic to Catalina Island, a single wild population exists, consisting of seven individuals in a canyon covering an area of approximately 250sqm. Rancho Santa Ana holds vegetatively propagated representatives of all seven individuals, as well as an eighth, cultivated plant, which is genetically different from the wild plants. Maintaining the complete set of known individuals provides the best hope of survival for this species in the wild by keeping future management options open.

Arizona is a haven for desert enthusiasts and two of the best places to become familiarized with the desert flora are the Desert Botanical Garden at Phoenix and the Arizona-Sonora Desert Museum. Established in 1939 by a small group of local residents, the Desert Botanical

beautiful gardens of the western world. His aim for the ranch land was to "preserve all the natural beauties of the place and establish as many domestic ornamentals and economic plants as could successfully be grown under California conditions". Today the garden includes a Japanese garden with a 19th-century Japanese house, an Australian garden, a water-lily garden, and a Shakespeare garden, featuring trees and flowers that appear in the plays. The most famous of the Huntington gardens is the desert garden, with a collection of cacti extending over more than four hectares. It was originally laid out in 1905 by a young German immigrant, William Hertrich, who shared Henry Huntington's vision for a world-class garden.

Garden has always aimed to encourage understanding and appreciation of the world's deserts, particularly the Sonoran Desert. The garden is located amid the red buttes of Papago Park, and consists of 20 hectares of attractive outdoor plantings. The Living Collection, which is especially strong in Cactaceae, Agavaceae and Aloaceae, consists of nearly 20,000 plants representing 3,886 taxa, and the garden is further renowned for its cactus collection, which includes more than 1,350 different taxa.

The conservation work of the Desert Botanical Garden is extremely important. Around 139 rare, threatened and endangered plant species are maintained by the garden, including 40 CPC National collection taxa. One of these is *Agave arizonica*, a plant first discovered in 1959 in the New River Mountains of Arizona, and one of the rarest and most beautiful of agaves. Its entire natural range is a small area in the centre of the State, where it grows on open rocky slopes in chaparral or juniper grassland at elevations between 1,100m and 2,750m. Cattle-grazing is a significant threat to the plant, as is illegal collection from the wild, which has been a major problem, especially given its slow growth rate and extremely low population numbers. Fortunately, the Desert Botanical Garden has successfully grown this plant both from seed and tissue culture and experimental attempts have been made to reintroduce plants to the wild.

Another threatened agave conserved by the garden is the Santa Cruz Striped Agave, *Agave parviflora*. This miniature species is highly attractive to collectors, and there now remain only around two dozen populations of *Agave parviflora* in southern Arizona, with additional populations in neighbouring parts of Mexico. As well as maintaining threatened plants in ex-situ collections, the Desert Botanical Garden has established permanent in-situ monitoring of sites and studies a range of threatened species in the wild.

An important feature of the Desert Botanical Garden is the Marshall Butterfly Pavilion, which provides information on the life cycle, migration and conservation of the Monarch butterfly, *Danaus plexippus*. One of the world's smallest migratory species, measuring just three inches from wing tip to wing tip, the Monarch may migrate up to 2,000 miles in its short lifespan. Very little is known about the migration behaviour of Monarch

Photo: Adam Rodriguez

*Agave parviflora* is threatened in the wild by mining and road construction, habitat degradation caused by grazing, and the impact of plant collectors.

butterflies in the southwest US. The garden is collaborating with the Boyce Thompson Arboretum to collect migration information through a tagging programme. The arboretum also encourages the creation of Monarch habitats by propagating native Arizona Milkweed – the Monarch's larval food – to be grown by schools and wildlife gardeners.

The Arizona-Sonora Desert Museum consists of a zoo, natural history museum and botanic garden, all at one 8.5-hectare desert site. Exhibits re-create the natural landscape of the Sonoran Desert Region with Mountain Lions, Prairie Dogs, Gila Monsters and more; altogether, the Museum has more than 300 animal species and 1,200 kinds of plants.

## CREEKS AND SPRINGS

Berry Botanic Garden in Portland, Oregon, is unusual among American botanic gardens in that, until comparatively recently, it was a private garden run by the talented and remarkable plantswoman, Rae Selling Berry, purely for her own pleasure and interest.

Rae and Alfred Berry moved to the site that is now the Berry Botanic Garden in 1938, acquiring a bowl-shaped site just north of Lake Oswego containing creeks and a ravine, springs, streams and a marsh. By this stage Rae Berry was already noted for her skills and enthusiasm for plants. In return for supporting plant collecting expeditions, many plant hunters, including Frank Kingdon-Ward and Joseph Rock, sent her seeds from their field trips, enabling her to raise an extraordinary collection of species rhododendrons and primulas. At the new garden she developed these collections and expanded them through seed exchange and correspondence.

Even as an elderly lady, Rae Berry could be found trekking through the Wallowa mountains in search of Oregon's *Primula cusikiana*. By the time of her death in 1976, aged 96, she had amassed a species garden that was known throughout the world. At the same time, she had left the creek and ravine areas untouched, allowing the native flora to thrive.

Today the garden is maintained by staff and volunteers and the main collections include primulas, rhododendrons, species lilies, alpines and native plants. After Mrs Berry's death, the garden collections were

carefully appraised. The discovery of 39 native alpine species by then rare or endangered in the wild (a perhaps unlooked-for result of her fascination with alpine plants) in the garden led to the establishment of a conservation programme. Since then the programme has expanded to include a wide range of native flora, and in 1983 a seed bank was set up to collect seed from endangered plants from the Pacific Northwest.

## THE HAWAIIAN ARCHIPELAGO: ISLANDS AND ATOLLS

Hawaii has an extraordinary flora and one that is under great threat. Located in the Pacific Ocean over 2,000 miles from the nearest continental land mass, the islands of Hawaii are the most isolated high islands in the world. This extreme isolation, together with a high diversity of habitat types, helps to explain the uniqueness of the flora, with more than 90 per cent of the native plants growing nowhere else in the world.

In total, about 1,500 plant species are native to Hawaii. Many of these are threatened with extinction as a result of deforestation, fires, overgrazing by introduced livestock and competition with invasive plant species. Nearly half of the 114 plant species known to have become extinct in the USA over the past 30 years were in Hawaii.

The National Tropical Botanical Garden (NTBG) is one of several agencies working hard to conserve Hawaii's rich flora. The garden implements an integrated strategy that tackles threats and recovery needs at the species and landscape levels, collecting plants for propagation in native plant nurseries, combined with ecological restoration and reserve management. It manages three botanic gardens in Hawaii together with areas of natural vegetation. Ex-situ and in-situ conservation techniques help ensure the long-term survival of the rare and threatened plants. Over the past 20 years, roughly two dozen species thought to be extinct have been rediscovered by NTBG botanists, and about 20 new species discovered that were unknown to science.

Concentrated conservation efforts are a priority for around 120 Hawaiian plant species that have fewer than 50 individuals remaining in the wild. These species are included in the so-called Genetic Safety Net (GSN) list. The NTBG has developed strict protocols for collecting

GSN plants from the wild as part of their recovery work. The protocols include genetic sampling of populations, recording accurate locations for individual plants and populations and the creation of high-quality maps showing species distribution. When the plants are brought into cultivation they are propagated by whatever means possible, to ensure that the number of individuals can be increased. If seed is available, this is stored to ensure the long term ex-situ conservation of the severely threatened species.

## Kauai

One of the natural areas managed by the National Tropical Botanic Garden is the Limahuli Preserve, which covers an area of 400 hectares. The 163-hectare Upper Valley of Limahuli is mostly intact and is home to a great abundance and exceptionally high diversity of native plants and animals. Among these are extant populations of ten plant species which are federally listed as threatened or endangered, as well as a large nesting colony of Newell's Shearwater (a pelagic seabird), Hawaiian Honey-creepers, Hawaiian Owls and the endemic Hoary Bat.

Since 1998, Limahuli Preserve has developed four hectares of lowland forest restoration outplanting sites, where about 5,000 native, nursery-grown trees and shrubs have been planted. A second major element crucial to the long-term protection of Limahuli is the construction of an ungulate-proof fence enclosing the entire Upper Valley of Limahuli, to keep feral pigs and goats from the Preserve. The endemic palm, *Pritchardia limahuliensis* is one of the species being protected by the Limahuli Preserve. Fewer than 100 individuals of this critically endangered palm tree are known from Limuhuli Valley where its natural habitat is lowland moist forest. Regeneration is limited, mainly because of seed predation by rats and pigs.

The headquarters of the National Tropical Botanic Garden is situated at the MacBryde Garden in the Lawai valley, on the west coast of Kauai. The Lawai Kai Coastal Restoration site is located at the mouth of Lawai Stream, on the south shore of Kauai. It is near paleocological and archaeological sites, which provide information on the local ecological history and which guided the restoration plan. A goal of this project is to improve coastal and lowland forest habitat for more than

Photo: National Tropical Botanic Garden, Hawaii

20 rare native plant species and to remove a thick mat of alien grass from the beach strand to enable sea turtles to nest. Several at-risk species are being planted within this site, including *Sesbania tomentosa*, *Munroidendron racemosum*, *Hibiscadelphus distans* and *Pritchardia aylmer-robinsonii*.

## Maui

Kahuna Garden, on the Hawaiian island of Maui, also forms part of the National Tropical Botanic Garden. It is situated on sacred land and includes a religious temple, the largest remaining ancient structure of Hawaii. The Kahuna garden is an ethnobotanical garden, explaining the relationships between people and the plants that are of significance in the local culture.

One of the special plant collections at Kahuna is the canoe garden featuring useful plants brought to Hawaii by Polynesian settlers approximately 2,000 years ago. Taro, *Colocasia esculenta*, for example, is a Polynesian plant introduction that is considered to be the cornerstone of traditional culture. According to mythology, the first Hawaiian was the younger sibling of the first taro plant. Every part of the taro plant can be eaten when cooked. The corms are eaten like potatoes or mashed, mixed with water and slightly fermented to make poi, the staple Hawaiian food.

Other important collections held at Kahuna include the Pacific collections of breadfruit and coconut, native Hawaiian plant species, and a native *Pandanus* forest.

Continuing the Hawaiian tradition of story-telling at Limahuli Preserve helps to convey the unqiue cultural and natural wealth of the area.

# BOTANIC GARDENS IN CANADA

Canada has 25 botanic gardens and in 1995 the Canadian Botanical Conservation Network was formed to promote the role of these gardens in conservation. Many of them manage natural areas, and over 1600 hectares of natural ecosystems are protected within land owned by the botanic gardens.

## THE ROYAL BOTANICAL GARDENS

The Royal Botanical Gardens is the largest botanic garden in Canada, taking in 122 hectares of cultivated garden and over 1,020 hectares of nature sanctuaries and wetlands, close to the city of Hamilton, Ontario. Since 1998 it has been designated a Site of National Historical and Architectural Significance. Thomas Baker McQuesten, a lawyer and Member of Provincial Parliament for the City of Hamilton, Ontario, originally conceived the idea for this garden. In the early 1920s, Canada had only two formal botanical institutions: the Central Experimental Farm in Ottawa, and the University of British Columbia's Botanical Garden in Vancouver. Motivated by a desire to develop and improve the city of Hamilton, McQuesten, then chairman for Public Works for the City, and C.V. Langs, chair of the City of Hamilton Board of Park Management, began the process of creating the garden at the northwestern entrance to the city. The first properties purchased by the city included 105 hectares of wooded land and 48.8 hectares of wetland called Westdale Park.

Key to the development of the park concept was the large Great Lakes coastal wetland called Cootes Paradise. Named after a British army officer stationed in the area at the time of the American Revolution, Cootes Paradise is a complex system of wetlands and ravines that extends inland from Hamilton Harbour, itself a bay of Lake Ontario. As early as 1887, civic and provincial governments were concerned to protect the marsh as a wildlife and bird sanctuary, and took steps to save it from filling and development. As a result, most of the marsh has remained intact.

In December 1929, the Parks Board gave approval to a suggestion that the name of Westdale Park should be changed to something more grand – Royal Botanical Gardens. This change was prompted by McQuesten, who was a frequent visitor to the Royal Botanic Gardens, Kew. In the same year, funding from the federal government allowed construction of a rock garden. As construction of the rock garden progressed, a royal charter was granted by King George V for use of the name Royal Botanical Gardens. Several other parcels of land were added to the growing park system in the years that followed.

The combination of cultivated public spaces and natural lands changed the original concept of Royal Botanical Gardens from that of a contained, cultivated showpiece to an outward-looking institution that included conservation and interpretation of natural habitats as part of its objectives. On 1 April 1941, management of the Royal Botanical Gardens was transferred to the Province of Ontario, the date being chosen to coincide with the centenary of the establishment of the Royal Botanic Gardens, Kew.

By 1950, the various properties within the Royal Botanical Gardens totalled 735 hectares. The last major parcel of property to come to Royal Botanical Gardens was more than 245 hectares of the Cootes Paradise Marsh, acquired in December 1977, giving Royal Botanical Gardens ownership of nearly all of Cootes

The Royal Botanical Gardens, Hamilton, preserves an important natural wetland area.

Photo: D. Galbraith/RBG Hamilton

Paradise, permitting extensive and integrated management of the marsh. Since 1950, management has involved controlling the population of invasive introduced Carp.

Today Royal Botanical Gardens' nature sanctuaries exhibit substantial biodiversity, with nearly 1,000 plant species, 25 species of mammal and 248 recorded bird species. Nearly 60 species of fish are present in the Cootes Paradise Marsh and adjacent waters. The rehabilitation of Cootes Paradise continues as one of Royal Botanical Gardens' most important projects; the wetland is one of the few remaining major spawning areas for native fish on the lower Great Lakes.

Five major cultivated garden areas now comprise the formal sections of Royal Botanical Gardens. The Arboretum occupies a site on the north shore of Cootes Paradise, with a Nature Interpretive Centre and horticultural plant propagation facilities. The Arboretum also houses the lilac collection. The Laking Garden is devoted to perennials, with major collections of iris and peony. The Rock Garden is now a historic site, and Hendrie Park has been developed to include several important theme gardens, including the Rose Garden, the World of Botany Garden, the Thyme Garden, the Woodland Garden and the Medicinal Plants Garden. Adjacent to Hendrie Park, RBG Centre includes the Mediterranean Garden Conservatory and the Children's Discovery Garden.

## NIAGARA PARKS

Thirteen miles north of the Canadian Horsehoe Falls lie the botanic gardens and horticulture school belonging to Ontario's Niagara Parks, a series of gardens, reserves and parks running alongside Niagara Falls and extending to the north. Originally established in 1936 as a School for Apprentice Gardeners, the campus was officially designated as a Botanical Garden in 1990. The gardens extend over 34 hectares and are maintained by the students at the School of Horticulture. The students also study at the Niagara Parks Greenhouses, and laboratory facilities in the Butterfly Conservatory are used for tissue culture and soil testing. The beautifully landscaped gardens include a herb garden, rock garden, vegetable plot, dwarf conifer collection and a fine arboretum with a range of ornamental trees and shrubs.

Photo: The Niagara Parks Commission

## A WORLD TOUR OF THE PLANT KINGDOM

The Jardin Botanique in Montreal is extensive, if not on the same scale as Royal Botanical Gardens, Ontario, with ten display glasshouses and 30 outdoor gardens set in a landscape of around 74 hectares. Of this land, about 40 hectares are devoted to an Arboretum with 7,000 specimens. The Japanese and Chinese gardens are popular attractions, while the glasshouses accommodate over 12,000 different species in themed areas, from the spiky vegetation of the Arid Regions house to colourful begonias, and gesneriads to feathery ferns, taking visitors on a virtual world tour of the plant kingdom. The Economic Tropical Plants Greenhouse gives visitors the chance to see over 125 of the plant species which provide the planet with food, fibres, spices, drugs and insecticides, from the cocoa trees from which we derive chocolate to spices like pepper and cinnamon, and crop plants such as bananas, coffee and figs.

Behind the public garden areas, research is carried out into afforestation and the restoration of degraded spaces. One project is investigating effective planting of abandoned farmland in Quebec with hardwoods of high commercial value. The quantity and quality of hardwood species are in decline in the forests of southern Québec, but disused farmland offers an opportunity to rebuild with high-value species. Other subject areas include environmental projects such as assessing the effectiveness of using aquatic plants to treat water, and conservation research into improving germination rates of temperate-zone orchids.

The Niagara Parks Garden has an important school of horticulture based on the teaching tradition at the Royal Botanic Gardens, Kew.

# Chapter 8

## LATIN AMERICA AND THE CARIBBEAN

Renowned for its lush vegetation and diverse flora, this region is famed as the source of many valuable plant species used as ornamentals, tropical crops, life-saving drugs and hardwood timbers. Today, biodiversity conservation is seen by botanic gardens as the most urgent priority.

The formerly abundant forests of Latin America and the larger Caribbean islands in particular have long been seen as a bountiful source of raw materials. With this resource now heavily depleted, botanic gardens have a vital role to play in cataloguing and researching the local flora and helping to conserve those species under threat. Throughout South America, botanic gardens are relatively few in number, given the extraordinary botanical richness of the continent and the growing conservation pressures. Nevertheless Argentina, Brazil and Colombia each have over 20 botanic gardens, and there are significant gardens on some Caribbean islands, each providing a valuable resource for study and enjoyment of the indigenous flora.

# BRAZILIAN GARDENS

Situated in the centre of Rio de Janeiro, the city's botanic garden, with its impressive avenues lined with Imperial Palms (*Roystonea oleracea*), provides a shady green oasis. The palms were planted at the time of the garden's inauguration in 1808. The garden was originally used to introduce cash crops such as tea, cloves, cinnamon and pineapples to Brazil. Now the emphasis has shifted to conservation and the Rio de Janeiro Botanic Garden, along with others in South America, has an important role to play in saving endangered plants from extinction. It remains a beautiful place to visit.

The natural vegetation of much of Rio de Janeiro State is Atlantic coastal forest or Mata Atlântica, one of the world's most species-rich and threatened ecosystems. This coastal area has been progressively deforested since Brazil's discovery by European settlers five hundred years ago, and now only about six per cent of the original coastal forest remains. Rio de Janeiro Botanic Garden Research Institute is actively involved in the study and conservation of the remnants of the forests of Rio de Janeiro State. Researchers from the garden have carried out surveys of the plants in the legally protected areas, such as the Poço das Antas Biological Reserve, which was set up to protect the endangered Golden Lion Tamarin, *Leonthoptecus rosalia*. The Poço das Antas Reserve vegetation consists of secondary forests patches surrounded by abandoned pastures. The frequent fires prevent natural regeneration and so the botanic garden has been helping the natural processes of forest recovery. The first step in ecological restoration was to identify which species occur naturally in the regeneration sites, and the second was to research how to produce seedlings of these species. Seed is also collected for ex-situ conservation purposes. The researchers also collect information about secondary succession, plant-animal interactions and tree phenology, to gain a good understanding of the ecology of secondary forest formations. After trials involving over 20 different species, those selected for initial replanting were species able to establish quickly and prevent invasive plants taking a hold. The Poço das Antas experience is now providing a model for the restoration of other degraded forest areas, such as the Tijuca National Park, an urban forest in Rio de Janeiro City.

In southern Brazil, the Botanic Garden of Curitiba is relatively new, created in 1991. It has been designed in the formal style of a French garden, the landscape dominated by a very attractive glasshouse. The whole city of Curitiba is renowned for its green image and the garden itself is involved in the conservation of the

PAGE 122: The 200-year-old Rio de Janeiro Botanic Garden has significant historic plantings such as these Imperial Palms. It also plays a major role in conserving Brazil's imperilled flora.

LEFT: The Atlantic coastal forest of Brazil is a global biodiversity hotspot. The Rio de Janeiro Botanic Garden is helping to conserve endemic trees and assist in forest regeneration.

southern portions of the Atlantic coastal forest, as well as promoting knowledge of the endangered plant resources in the Araucaria pine forest in the State of Paraná. As part of this work botanists are studying the local flora and helping with conservation assessments, passing on the information to national and international institutions. They are also helping to design a strategy for the management of existing and new conservation areas, and helping to educate the public.

## CAATINGA: CACTI AND SUCCULENT BROMELIADS

In addition to the Atlantic coastal forest region, Brazil has botanic gardens in various major ecological regions of the country. The Jardim Botânico da Fundacão Zoobotânica de Belo Horizonte, in Minas Gerais State, for example, is located in the semi-arid northeast of the country, where there is a large area of seasonally dry, deciduous thorn forest. This low, dense vegetation, known as caatinga, covers ten per cent of the country, in an area with very low and irregular rainfall, in some years receiving scarcely any rain at all. Where the rainfall is highest and soils relatively deep, caatinga forest occurs, a form of seasonal tropical broadleaved forest. More typical, however, is a form of shrubby caatinga known as carrasco. In drier areas cacti and succulent bromeliads form an important part of the vegetation. Some of the local cacti, such as *Cereus jamacaru*, *Pereskia grandifolia* and *Pereskia bahiensis* are used to create living impenetrable fences for livestock or to form hedges around homesteads.

The caatinga vegetation generally is becoming increasingly degraded and threatened as a result of extensive cattle-rearing and charcoal production, and many of the endemic species of this region are now considered endangered. Some of the species are under the added threat of over-exploitation. Endemic cactus species *Discocactus*, *Uebelmannia* and *Melocactus* have suffered heavily as a result of commercial collection for the international market.

The Belo Horizonte garden is studying and helping to conserve the local caatinga vegetation. An important component of this is an educational programme to inform visitors to the garden and local communities of the ecological and cultural importance of the caatinga.

Rare cacti are being propogated in Belo Horizonte as part of an integrated conservation programme.

Photo: R. Wasum

Surveys have been carried out of plants in their natural habitats and how they are used by local people. Various species, including critically endangered cacti such as *Coleocephalocereus purpureus* and *Pilocereus azulensis,* are now being cultivated to aid their long-term survival and for educational displays – seeds from cultivated plants have also been distributed for use by local schools. The greenhouse at the botanic garden has been redeveloped to house an educational exhibit aimed specifically at raising awareness of the social and cultural importance of the unique plants of the caatinga, the people they support and the threats they face.

The construction of the Botanic Garden in Belo Horizonte is relatively recent; the Fundacão Zoobotânica de Belo Horizonte was established in 1991 and the garden was created soon afterwards. The building of the physical structure began in 1996, with the construction of the plant nursery. This was followed by the central greenhouse and four small greenhouses, designed by the famous Brazilian architect, Oscar Niemeyer. The addition of the garden to the existing zoo fulfils the original intention of establishing a Zoo-Botanic Garden in the city. The new botanic garden is the first one in Minas Gerais State and is dedicated to improving knowledge of the regional flora, with a specific focus on threatened species and their habitats.

The Botanic Garden of Salvador is carrying out a different role in relation to its local environment. The botanic garden in this vibrant and historic city, once Brazil's main slave port, is researching the plants which form part of Afro-Brazilian culture, and is developing environmental educational programmes based on the ethnobotanical information derived from the project. The uses of over 40 plant species related to Afro-Brazilian culture were investigated in the urban parks and botanical gardens of Salvador; over 80 per cent of these species have medicinal properties, and some others have edible, ornamental and industrial uses. The research has also provided very valuable information about the sacred plants used in Candomblé, a popular religious cult which recognizes the Orixás spirits who link people with their creator-god Olorum.

# COLOMBIA

Colombia has a network of 21 botanic gardens located in different regions of the country, and an additional ten gardens are planned. The Jardín Botánico José Celestino Mutis in Bogotá is named after José Celestino Mutis, the Spanish botanist who was born in Cadiz in 1732 and died in Santa Fe de Bogote in 1808. After studying mathematics and then medicine, Mutis became professor of anatomy in Madrid, where he became acquainted with Linnaeus. Linnaeus later gave him the sobriquet "*phytologorum americanorum princeps*" ("the Prince of American botanists") and named several plants in his honour, including the genus Mutisia. In 1760 Mutis was appointed physician to Don Pedro Mesia de la Cerda, the Viceroy of New Granada, and later became professor of mathematics in the College of Nuestra Señora del Rosario. He spent 40 years working on the *Flora de Nueva Granada*, during which time he distinguished various species of cinchona. He also discovered and classified important medicinal plants such as *Psychotria ipecacuanha*.

The Jardín Botánico José Celestino Mutis was established in 1955. Its aims are the study, conservation and sustainable use of the Andean flora. Within the grounds there are plantings representing the most important Andean ecosystems, found at altitudes of 2,000m–3,800m: páramo, woodland, wetlands and arid vegetation. There are also glasshouses containing tropical plants from lowland areas of Colombia, together with medicinal plant collections. The garden is also considered a valuable refuge for birds, with around 25 per cent of all the bird species occurring in the Bogotá region having been recorded in the gardens.

RIGHT: Cacti and succulents at the Jardín Botánico José Celestino Mutis.

BELOW: A species of *Mandevilla*, a tropical woody vine growing in the Jardín.

Photo: Jardín Botánico José Celestino Mutis

Photo: Jardín Botánico José Celestino Mutis

# ARGENTINA

Argentina's network of botanic gardens continues to expand and the gardens are beginning to broaden their appeal by reaching out to the public. In 2005, Argentina celebrated its first National Botanic Gardens Day, with special events held throughout the country. The Carlos Thays Municipal Botanical Garden is a small garden, situated right in the heart of Buenos Aires. Established in 1898, it is Argentina's oldest botanic garden.

The Castelar Botanic Garden is situated close to Buenos Aires and was established in 1947. The main purpose of this garden was the acclimatization of new plants, but now education and conservation are becoming increasingly important. The garden is currently being restored (see pp.143–144).

Elsewhere in Argentina, small botanic gardens are generally attached to universities and have been used mainly for formal teaching purposes. In contrast, the newly created Jardín Botánico del Chaco Arido, established in May 2004 as the first garden in La Rioja Province, has broader aims; this garden is working on recording the native plant diversity in the dry woodland habitats of the region, cultivating plants for conservation purposes and promoting environmental education.

The Carlos Thays Municipal Botanic Garden in Buenos Aires.

Photo: BGCI

# CHILE: PRAIRIE TO RAINFOREST

Chile has nine botanic gardens. The Valdivia Botanic Garden, one of the most southerly botanic gardens in the world, was established in 1955, at the same time as the Southern University of Chile (Universidad Austral de Chile), of which it forms a part. The garden is situated on an island in the basin of the Valdivia river, and its ten hectares are laid out to display different plant formations of central Chile, with forest areas, scrubland, swamps and prairies. The Valdivian rainforest, a natural feature of the coastal and Andean mountain ranges, is particularly well represented in the garden. The principal genus of this temperate rainforest is *Nothofagus*, of which there are three dominant evergreen species: *N. dombeyi*, *N. nitida* and *N. betuloides*.

The Instituto de Investigaciones Agropecuarias (INIA) of Chile is working with Kew on a project of ex-situ conservation of endemic, vulnerable and endangered plant species from desert and Mediterranean zones of the country. Collecting, joint research and a continuing training programme are central to the project, which will be seeking to form additional academic and technical partnerships with institutions throughout central and northern Chile as it develops. The Chilean fieldwork team is initially concentrating on threatened geophytes, and will move on to endangered tree and shrub species from central Chile. The project involves collecting information on the biology and ecology of native species, especially focusing on seed and fruit characteristics, germination, dispersal and pollination.

# MEXICO: CACTI AND AGAVES

OPPOSITE: The UNAM Botanic Garden in Mexico City is closely associated with the study of Mexico's rich flora and also provides welcome green space in a crowded urban environment.

Many of the species grown around the world as ornamentals come from the rich flora of Mexico: familiar examples include the dahlia, zinnia and sunflower, but above all, cacti – plants which perhaps more than any other evoke this country of extensive dryland areas. In total, Mexico has over 900 species of cacti, more than any other country in the world, and it is estimated that around 75 per cent of these species are endemic to the country. Sadly, however, nearly 200 Mexican cacti species are threatened with extinction in the wild. All Mexican cacti have been protected by national legislation for over 60 years, but this has not prevented smuggling across the border into the USA, and further afield to Europe and Japan. Other threats include habitat modification and destruction. Botanic gardens play a very important role in helping to conserve the diversity of Mexico's succulent flora and, as far as possible, restoring species of cacti and other succulents to their natural habitats.

Some of the endangered Mexican cacti are known as living rock cacti, the small and slow-growing cacti of the genus *Ariocarpus*, well camouflaged in their arid, rocky habitats of the Chihuahua Desert. Although demand for cacti has never reached the same pitch as the 19th century orchid craze, avid collectors have long sought rare and unusual species. One of the most endangered species of living rock cacti is *Ariocarpus agavoides*, which grows in a very restricted area in the State of Tamaulipas at the edge of the Chihuahuan desert. It has been heavily depleted by collection for the international market and now the expansion of a nearby urban area and the dumping of rubbish threaten the survival of this precious little plant. As yet there is no botanic garden in Chihuahua, but there are plans to create one with a strong emphasis on conservation.

Another important group of Mexican succulent plants are the agaves. These plants with their succulent leaves are important to the rural economy, both as a source of fibre such as sisal and for the production of alcoholic drinks, the most famous of which is tequila (from *Agave tequilana*). Other species are also harvested from the wild for the illicit production of mescal – another alcoholic beverage.

Photo: BGCI

*Echeveria* is a large genus of succulents in the Crassulaceae family, with many species native to Mexico.

One of the most impressive botanic gardens in Mexico is the Jardín Botánico del Instituto de Biología, Universidad Nacional Autónoma (UNAM), in Mexico City. This botanic garden has an area of ten hectares, a major portion of which is dedicated to the Mexican cactus expert, Dr. Helia Bravo-Hollis. The succulent collection includes the Mexican national collection of agaves, with over 140 species of the Agavaceae family and over 450 species of cacti. Researchers at the garden are actively involved in the conservation of succulent plants in their natural habitats. In 1990, UNAM conducted a rescue operation in the Río Moctezuma valley to save the habitat of the Golden Barrel Cactus, *Echinocactus grusonii*, prior to a major dam project. Most of the habitat of this species has been destroyed,

but it is well known in cultivation and can be seen in many botanic gardens. UNAM has also been actively involved in the conservation of the Tehuacán-Cuicatlán valley, between the States of Puebla and Oaxaca, one of the most important sites in Mexico for cactus diversity, with many different tree cacti. UNAM has studied the valley in detail and identified the most important site for habitat protection. When a major highway was built through the valley, UNAM relocated specimens of about 50 different species and distributed them to botanic gardens for safe keeping. The 40-plus botanic gardens in Mexico are linked through the Association of Mexican Botanic Gardens, which was formed in 1983.

The Jardín Botánico Francisco Javier Clavijero is named in honour of the 18th-century Jesuit monk and historian, who was born in Veracruz but died in exile. He had a great love and respect for nature and for the Indian cultures of Mexico. The garden covers approximately 7.5 hectares in Xalapa, the state capital of Veracruz. Early development of this garden was assisted by Royal Botanic Gardens, Kew, and it was opened in 1977. The garden is situated on the windward slopes of the Sierra Madre Oriental, in an area of disturbed cloudforest with relatively high rainfall and frequent mists. The garden is naturally landscaped and includes a wooded hillside rich in native trees and shrubs. Other areas of the garden include ornamental plantings with a pond, a 'useful plants' section, palmetum, arboretum and pinetum, with plenty to interest the visitor and with added educational potential. There are two exhibition greenhouses, one for mostly native tropical rainforest species and the other for cacti, succulents and other arid zone plants. Plants on display here include the Barrel Cactus *Echinocactus platyacanthus*, and the columnar *Neobuxbaumia tetetzo* from the Tehuacan valley, as well as the Tequila Agave, *Agave tequilana*.

The overall focus of the Jardín Botánico Francisco Javier Clavijero is very much on the study and conservation of Mexico's rich native flora, with an emphasis on the threatened and endangered species. As the garden is an integral part of the Instituto de Ecologia, it is supported by wider research resources, including a herbarium containing approximately 230,000 specimens. This is considered to be one of Mexico's most important herbaria.

# CLOUDFOREST

The cloudforests of eastern Mexico consist of a unique and diverse mix of temperate and tropical species. Some of the temperate species have affinities with the vegetation of the southeastern USA, with genera such as *Liquidambar*, *Carpinus*, *Ostrya*, *Quercus* and *Clethra*. Common tropical elements include the trees *Cedrela*, *Meliosma*, *Oreopanax*, *Podocarpus* together with tree ferns, *Cyathea*, and palms, *Chamaedorea*. The cloudforest display area of the garden Jardín Botánico Francisco Javier Clavijero can be explored via paths and steps which disturb the habitat as little as possible and enable visitors to see the plants growing as they would in the wild. This display includes ancient trees covered with epiphytes such as *Tillandsia*, many orchids, ferns, and *Lycopodium*, which were growing on the site when the garden was first established. Alongside these are native plants introduced from other cloudforest remnants, now regenerating naturally in this area, including the understorey palms, *Chamaedorea tepejilote* and the threatened *C. klotzschiana*, and ferns, especially the endangered *Marattia laxa* and the rare *Psilotum complanatum* that only grows in association with tree ferns. There have been propagation programmes since 1990 for threatened cloudforest trees such as *Symplocos coccinea*, *Podocarpus guatemalensis* and *Styrax glabrescens*. Rescue and propagation of two

Photo: Antony Challenger

endangered species, *Magnolia dealbata* and *Talauma mexicana*, has been a success story for the garden; seed storage and propagation techniques were developed and the species was established in cultivation for the first time. Seedlings have been reintroduced into the adjoining ecological park as well as distributed to state and municipal nurseries as future seed trees for the propagation of the species.

Another conservation success of the Jardín Botánico Francisco Javier Clavijero has involved the commercial cultivation of a cycad, *Dioon edule.* As well as suffering habitat destruction, this species has been subject to illegal collection of leaf crowns. Working with local farmers has resulted in a small nursery dedicated to the propagation of this cycad from seed. This nursery is registered with the authorities under the condition that the farmers protect the natural habitat of the cycad and discourage illegal removal of plants. Reintroduction of nursery-produced seedlings will be undertaken in order to compensate for seed removal from the habitat.

In a similar way the garden is also working with local women to promote conservation and sustainable use of biodiversity. The aim is to use organic cultivation to diversify the production of useful plants, based on the traditional knowledge of peasant women in rural communities south of the Cofre de Perote area of Veracruz.

Photo: Antony Challenger

# BELIZE: ORCHIDS AND PALMS

The Belize Botanic Gardens were established on land that had been cleared for agriculture when it was purchased by two visionary individuals, Ken and Judy du Plooy, in 1989. An adjacent and also degraded tract of land on the Macal River was acquired five years later. Both sites were restored, and the Belize Botanic Gardens were officially registered in 1997. Belize has a particularly rich orchid flora and therefore the cultivation and study of orchids is a particular focus of the garden. *Encyclia cochleata*, the national flower of Belize and one of the few Belizean orchids that flowers nearly all the year round, is one of the many species held by the botanic gardens. Since 1997 a collaboration with the National Botanic Gardens, Glasnevin, in Ireland, has resulted in 20 orchid species being added to the known orchid flora of Belize, including one newly discovered species.

OPPOSITE: An aerial view of the Belize Botanic Gardens.

RIGHT: Belize Botanic Gardens are home to an impressive collection of native orchids, including this species, *Mormoles buccinator*.

Photo: Brett Adams

The Belize Botanic Gardens also maintain a palm collection with almost all the 40 native palm species of the country in cultivation, together with 50 palm species from elsewhere in the world. Several threatened species from Cuba are in cultivation, providing an ex-situ conservation resource in case the plants in Cuba are lost through, for example, hurricane or disease. The Gardens promote agricultural diversity as well as conservation of the native flora; one example of this is the work on the Bay Leaf Palm, *Sabal maritiiformis*, which is used for thatch roofing by the Belizean Maya and Mestizo, and increasingly in tourism developments. A demonstration plot of 1,500 Bay Leaf Palms has been established in the garden for research purposes and for observation by farmers. In the wild, the palm species is becoming scarce as a result of habitat loss and overcollection for thatching, but farming provides a sustainable alternative to wild collection; the palm is an ideal sustainable agriculture crop for most areas of Belize as it requires little or no irrigation or pest control in its natural areas of distribution and there is a ready demand. Belize Botanic Gardens is planning to make information and seeds available to potential farmers in the near future.

## HURRICANE-RESISTANT PLANTS

Hurricanes provide a major challenge to botanic gardens in the Caribbean region, and some of these challenges were addressed at a *Caribbean Botanic Gardens for Conservation* conference, held at Belize Botanic Gardens in 2005. Ironically, while participants were discussing the importance of planning for hurricanes, the Dr Alfredo Marín Barrier Botanic Garden in Mexico was being destroyed as the eye of hurricane Wilma passed overhead. The same storm caused a massive baobab tree to be uprooted at the Kampong of the National Tropical Botanic Garden in Florida. The baobab joined 46 other Kampong trees that had been propped up after hurricane Katrina. With this reality in mind, the Caribbean Botanic Garden Network decided to work together to assist with garden recovery operations and to identify hurricane-resistant plants that might be able to withstand this annual threat.

Photo: Mike Green

# CUBA: A RICH ENDEMIC FLORA

Cuba has a fine tradition of botanical research and appreciation of plants. Within the country there are 11 botanic gardens which work together to help conserve the rich flora of the island. The National Network of Cuban Botanic Gardens was created in 1990 by a decree of the President of the Academy of Sciences. Cuban botanic gardens are increasingly involved in the evaluation of human impact on natural ecosystems, in the preparation of floristic surveys of important natural sites for conservation, and also in designing and developing environmental education programmes.

Cuba has a complex and ancient natural history, with a rich endemic flora resulting from its geographical position, its isolation, varied topography and wide variety of soil types. In total there are about 6,700 vascular plant species with an endemism of about 50 per cent. As with all the Caribbean islands, Cuba's natural ecosystems have been heavily modified over the last two or three centuries and today only 14 per cent of the island is covered by primary vegetation, mainly located in the mountains. Cuba has about 960 threatened plant species, 87 per cent of which grow only in Cuba.

The first botanical garden in Cuba was inaugurated on 30 May 1817 under the direction of Jose Antonio de la Ossa, who collected plants from the areas surrounding the city of Havana. He established a garden with orange trees, walnuts, oaks, rosebushes and tropical fruit trees, and also cultivated medicinal plants, providing leaves, roots and fruits to the drugstores of Havana.

Today the National Botanic Garden of Cuba, situated in the south of Havana, is an extensive and magnificent garden. Established in 1968, it covers an area of approximately 600 hectares and plays an important role in conservation and environmental education. The various Cuban vegetation types are represented, work which began in 1969. Today there are well-established examples of dry forest, rainforest, pine forest and the very special mogote and serpentine vegetation, in an area covering 120 hectares. Mogote, or haystack mountain vegetation, grows naturally in areas of limestone karst in two separate areas of Cuba. In the western part of the country the Mogote forests are particularly rich and 40 per cent of the plants are unique to that small area.

## CONSERVING CUBAN PALMS

Palm species are extremely important in the biodiversity of Cuba. There are over a hundred species, the majority of which are

*Coccothrinax bordhiana* is one of Cuba's 'Critically Endangered' species of palm. Seen here growing in the wild, it is also in cultivation in the National Botanic Garden of Cuba in Havana.

Photo: Miguel Angel Vales

endemic to the island. The National Botanic Garden has a first-class collection of different species and is actively involved in promoting palm conservation. The garden has recently been involved in the Cuban Palm Project, in collaboration with other gardens in the Cuban network, as part of the Global Trees Campaign, a joint initiative of FFI, BGCI and UNEP-WCMC. Experts from the gardens have assessed the conservation status and threats to some of the rarest palm species, and developed strategies to save them from extinction. Field work confirmed that one of the palms studied, *Coccothrinax crinita,* is critically endangered. This species, which is confined to Pinar del Río Province, is now reduced to 130 individuals in the wild found only at two localities, in dry semi-deciduous secondary forest. *Coccothrinax crinita* has many uses for local people; the leaves and fibres are used to make brushes, hats and stuffing for pillows and mattresses, the trunks are used in the construction of houses, and the fruits are used as animal feed. Overexploitation is a threat to this palm, as are cattle grazing, burning and the impact of invasive species. The number of individuals has declined by over 50 per cent in the last 30 years.

In-situ conservation, propagation studies undertaken in the botanic gardens, reintroduction and public education are all important components of the conservation strategy for *C. crinita*. Specimens are being planted in prominent places, such as in the grounds of health centres and in the recreational park in the Bahía Honda municipality, and a Managed Flora Reserve has been created to protect this critically endangered palm species in its natural habitat. The Reserve also works to protect other threatened trees, such as *Buxus* spp., box trees, which grow at the same forest site.

As well as carrying out essential conservation work, the National Botanic Garden of Cuba provides an educational and community resource with a focus on useful plants. The garden is directly helping to improve the diets and self-sufficiency of Cubans and contains one of Cuba's very few vegetarian restaurants. The garden's fruit tree project is developing species and varieties of tropical fruit trees specifically for the Havana climate and soil types. Over 35 varieties of mango are in cultivation, together with all the common citrus fruits and many other less common species. The garden provides interpretative materials to educate the public about the value of cultivating a diverse selection of organic plants, and is able to advise on planting appropriate for small gardens or back yards.

# ST VINCENT

Elsewhere in the Caribbean, the St Vincent Botanic Gardens remains an historic landmark of major national, regional and global significance. Conservation of rare plant species has been practised since the garden was first established in 1764. It now occupies approximately eight hectares about one mile outside the capital, Kingstown, and trained guides give garden tours, explaining the medicinal values of plants, and their places of origin. The Nicholas Wildlife Aviary Complex, located within the gardens, plays a vital conservation role as part of the captive breeding programme to save the endangered St Vincent Parrot, *Amazona guildingii*.

Throughout Latin America botanic gardens are committed to the study and conservation of the rich and diverse flora of the region. The gardens work in partnership within national and regional botanic garden networks and in collaboration with national parks and other protected areas. Many of the botanic gardens have developed close conservation partnerships with institutions in other parts of the world. The Missouri Botanical Garden works closely with gardens, universities and other research institutes in Bolivia, Ecuador, Peru, Nicaragua and Panama for example; the Royal Botanic Gardens, Kew has longstanding connections with botanical research in Brazil, and the Royal Botanic Gardens Edinburgh helps with the conservation of the conifers of Chile. Conserving the megadiversity from Mexico to Tierra del Fuego, with around 120,000 plant species, requires a truly international effort.

# Chapter 9

## LOOKING AHEAD – BOTANIC GARDENS IN THE 21ST CENTURY

Botanic gardens have continually adapted in response
to changing needs, their development reflecting advances
in science as well as wider changes in society. Botanic gardens
are today broadening their relevance once again to help tackle
global issues such as sustainable development, poverty
alleviation, loss of biodiversity and climate change.

The earliest botanic gardens were devoted to the study and teaching of medicinal plants at a time when medicine and botany were one science. Botanic gardens later became hugely important as centres for the dissemination of plant species of economic value and for the development of agriculture, particularly in the tropics. The amenity and recreational significance of botanic gardens grew in importance during the 19th century, particularly with the growth of major cities in Europe and North America and the increased interest shown in domestic gardening by the wealthy and influential middle classes. In more recent decades the conservation of rare and threatened species has become a fundamental aim of botanic gardens, inspired by growing awareness of the loss of plant species around the world.

# NEW GARDENS

The global network of botanic gardens continues to grow and reflect new demands. About half of all the botanic gardens of the world have been created since 1950, and since 1990 more than a hundred new botanic gardens have been developed. The Eden Project in the UK has been a phenomenal success, inspiring a new generation with a passion for gardening and a respect for, and appreciation of, plants generally. In China, at a time of rapid development, new botanic gardens are being created and well-established gardens are reaching out to the public. The Chinese Academy of Sciences and the Beijing municipal government are planning to build a world-class botanic garden as a showcase for the country's rich plant diversity and for the research capabilities of its botanists. At a recent meeting to mark the 50th anniversary of the Beijing Botanical Garden, it was announced that this garden would be transformed to become the national botanic garden of China.

The Nezahat Gökyigit Botanic Garden (NGBG) in Istanbul, Turkey, is an example of a newly created garden which combines the recreational, educational, scientific and conservation roles of a botanic garden. This is a unique 50-hectare botanic garden situated on formerly derelict land at a busy motorway intersection in a residential area of Istanbul, and is now the largest replanted green area in this huge city. Originally started in 1995 by a wealthy businessman as a memorial park dedicated to his late wife, in April 2003 the park became the Nezahat Gökyigit Botanic Garden, its aim "to explore, explain and conserve the world's plants".

This garden is being developed in a city which, in view of the richness of the local flora, has relatively few arboreta or botanic gardens. Gökyigit Botanic Garden will have a conservation function, to protect endemic and rare plants of the Istanbul area, which are severely threatened by rapid urban development, and generally to help care for Turkey's rich and varied flora, comprising over 9,000 taxa, one third of which are endemic. Advice on developing the garden has been sought from overseas, and there are regular visits by experts from such gardens as the Royal Botanic Gardens, Kew and Edinburgh.

Since 1995, more than 50,000 trees and shrubs from 150 different species have been planted, although not all have survived the challenging conditions of a previously degraded site. Since 2003, all new plant accessions have been added to a plant database. Geophytes (plants with bulbs, corms or tubers) are one speciality, representing the rich diversity of allium, tulip, lily, snowdrop, anemone, iris and cyclamen species that are native to Turkey. In the 21 bulb frames, an extensive collection of over 250 geophytes from 36 genera of plants has been created, in pots sunk into raised beds made from old railway sleepers. The bulbs have all been collected from the wild during the past few years and carefully documented to form the basis of a conservation collection. The collection is a very valuable resource, not only for display and for educating the public, but also for propagation, research and reintroduction to the wild.

So far only one area of the garden has been developed, but there are plans for expansion. In the first new area to be developed, on the highest point of the garden, there is a gazebo from which visitors can look out over the grounds. From here a water cascade flows down to ornamental ponds. In springtime, visitors can see such plants as galanthus, cyclamen, crocus, narcissus, iris and tulips in flower. Hundreds of bulbs have been planted throughout the garden, giving colourful displays from February through to May. Near to the bulb frames is a rock garden with scree area, and a recently created crevice garden which looks at its best in the spring. Between the two ponds is a wooden pergola which during May and June is heavy with the scent of climbers, such as roses, *Trachelospermum*, jasmine and honeysuckle. Later in the year there are lilies, dahlias and hydrangeas. There is also a productive vegetable and fruit garden with mulberry, cherry, apricot and peach trees and raspberries, blackberries, tayberries and grape vines.

A second area, through a tunnel under the motorway, is being landscaped, with planting schemes along the garden paths for displaying native species from all over Turkey. A medicinal plant collection is also under construction.

In 2005, a new education building was opened, where summer school courses are held for children from

PAGE 138: The Eden Project in Cornwall, UK, is immensely successful at introducing a new audience to botanic gardens and at explaining the global importance of plants.

BELOW: The Nezahat Gökyigit Botanic Garden in Istanbul demonstrates what can be achieved in a derelict urban area and is catalysing conservation action for the wider countryside.

*Dracaena cinnabari,* an endemic and threatened tree on the tiny island of Socotra is being cultivated at the fledgling botanic garden being developed there with support from the Royal Botanic Garden, Edinburgh.

local schools, together with lectures and workshops bringing together botanic garden staff from throughout Turkey and overseas. A children's garden is also planned, where local schools can learn to grow and maintain their own flowers and vegetables. To raise awareness of the increasing problem of water scarcity, there are plans for an area devoted to plants which will tolerate arid conditions and which can be useful in the global struggle against soil erosion and desertification. Recycling is seen as an important aspect of the garden and a composting system has been established to obtain a natural organic fertilizer to improve soil fertility.

In Jordan, an even younger botanic garden is taking shape. In March 2005, HRH Prince Faisal, the Regent, of Jordan inaugurated the first national botanic garden in the kingdom, a site of 100 hectares in a country park at Tel el Ruman, 15 miles from the capital, Amman. The area is one of outstanding natural beauty, already rich in wild flowers, and overlooking the King Talal Dam. The Royal Botanic Garden of Jordan will be a regional centre for native plant conservation, public education and scientific research, and will have links with other gardens, both in the region and worldwide. Jordan is a country with a particularly rich flora; despite its small size, it is home to diverse habitats with over 2,000 different plant species, some of which are unique to Jordan. As elsewhere, this biodiversity is under threat from urbanisation, poor land management and population growth. Only limited scientific research has been done on this flora, and there are likely to be plants in the country still unknown to science.

The Royal Botanic Garden is envisaged as having one principal site, with the development of a number of satellite gardens in the future, to display and conserve some of the habitats and indigenous plants in different parts of the country. There are also plans for a smaller garden of about two hectares, in the coastal city of Aqaba, which will specialize in tropical plants.

A fledgling botanic garden has been created on the Indian Ocean island of Socotra. This island has a remarkable succulent plant flora with many endemic species threatened by overgrazing. A small nursery was established in 1996, initially to grow tomatoes and other food crops. The father and son who ran the nursery soon turned their attention to the cultivation of Socotra's endemic plants and they have achieved major successes. The Socotran Cucumber Tree, *Dendroscycios socotrana,* and Dragon's Blood Tree, *Dracaena cinnabari*, are two species that have thrived in the nursery and its tiny associated garden. Socotra is beginning to open up to tourism and the botanic garden may become a good place to learn about the island's extraordinary flora. An immediate need for the garden, however, is a strong perimeter fence to prevent the ravages of grazing goats.

Looking ahead, a new botanic garden is under development in Oman. Situated 27 miles from Muscat, the Oman Botanic Park is being developed as a centre for biodiversity conservation, education and environmental tourism. Enclosed by low hills to the north and mountains to the south, the garden will be developed on an area of limestone gravel outwash and low hills with *Acacia* woodland. The documented living collection of native plants will reflect the many different habitat types found in Oman, from the monsoon cloud-forest in the far south of the country, with its endemic plant species, to the vegetation of the sand dunes and salt flats. Plants used in traditional agricultural systems, such as the important date gardens, will be displayed.

However, botanic gardens will also be needed in other parts of the world, to act as resource centres for plant conservation and sustainable development and to demonstrate the fundamental importance of plants. Countries in the Middle East and Asia which do not yet have a botanic garden include Lebanon, Syria, Afghanistan, Cambodia and Laos; in Africa, the Central African Republic, Congo and Eritrea; and in the Pacific Islands, Micronesia, New Caledonia and Vanuatu.

There is, thankfully, real interest in developing new gardens. Kabul University in Afghanistan, for example, is planning to landscape its walled grounds as a basis for the future development of a botanic garden. This is seen, in the first instance, as a safe haven and pleasant environment for the students and wider community, providing respite from the war-torn city. A later development phase would be to cultivate and study the economic potential of Afghanistan's rich flora as an aid to rural development.

# GARDEN RESTORATION

It is a sad fact that botanic gardens can fall into disrepair in times of war or economic hardship, when priorities are understandably elsewhere. Various botanic gardens in tropical Africa, for example, and in parts of the former Soviet Union, are in need of repair. Restoration is beginning in some of these gardens in an attempt to return them to their former glory. One example is the Calabar Botanic Garden in Nigeria. Not only does Nigeria have the largest population of any African country, but it also has some of the worst environmental problems. Deforestation is a major issue; the remaining ten per cent of Nigeria's rich rainforest is largely confined to the Cross River State and is one of the five geographical centres for biodiversity in Africa. The botanic garden in Calabar, the capital of Cross River State, could play a major role in conserving medicinal and other economic plants from a threatened rainforest area of global importance.

The Calabar Botanic Garden was established in 1893 by the Royal Botanic Gardens, Kew. Over the years, management came under the control of the Cross River State Forestry Department which converted the garden into a zoo in the 1970s but the grounds then fell into disrepair. In more recent years the Forestry Department and environmental groups in Calabar have discussed various ideas for the rehabilitation of the garden, and these ideas are now being converted into action. It is hoped the garden will demonstrate and conserve the threatened flora of the area, and attract tourists to this rich rainforest region. There are also plans for the garden to serve the needs of the local community, by propagating useful and over-exploited trees of the region and distributing them to local villages.

In the late 1940s, a botanic garden was established in Argentina by Arturo E. Ragonese, for the introduction and acclimatization of plants. Situated in Castelar, not far from Buenos Aires, the garden developed a unique collection of about 3,500 plant taxa, providing material for research on taxonomy, plant breeding, phytochemistry, and potential uses of plants. Ragonese was an ardent botanical explorer who travelled extensively throughout the country, collecting herbarium material and timber samples and studying natural plant communities. In 1997, after years of abandonment under a failed private administration, a project for its revival was launched and this is now being fully implemented. New offices, laboratory and a visitor centre are being developed, the living plant collections restored, and conservation and environmental education programmes established. For the first time the botanic garden will be open to the public. It has

great potential as a visitor attraction, situated about 20 miles west of Buenos Aires, and is planned to become one of the few and invaluable "green lungs" and biological reserves in the region of Buenos Aires, the region with the highest population density in the country. The different vegetation types of Argentina will be represented, such as the pampas grassland, the Chaco dry broadleaf forest and savannah, and rainforest. Among the collections will be useful plants, including timber, forage, aromatic, edible and ornamental species, reflecting the historic interests of the garden.

Photo: BGCI

# BOTANIC GARDENS AND SUSTAINABLE DEVELOPMENT

Well-established gardens with a strong suit in biodiversity conservation are increasingly examining their role in linking natural resources with human needs. In a way they are returning to their roots, as centres which relate the diversity of plants to healthcare and food crop development. The concept of linking natural resources with human needs was expressed in Stockholm in 1972, at the UN Conference on the Human Environment. Since then, the idea has been developed and incorporated by many major international policies concerned with both poverty and the environment, and was most recently and prominently emphasized by the World Summit for Sustainable Development (WSSD) held in Johannesburg in 2002. The WSSD developed an ambitious plan to accelerate the transition to sustainable development. The targets set within this global plan build on the Millennium Development Goals (MDGs), a set of eight ambitious goals for tackling poverty which were agreed at the UN Millennium Summit in 2000. They represent an unprecedented commitment by the international community to tackling the persistent problems of human deprivation, and recognize the importance of a healthy environment in achieving this: one of the key goals is for environmental sustainability.

The main mechanism linking the work of botanic gardens to the big development agenda is the Global Strategy for Plant Conservation (GSPC) (see page 151). This Strategy, with its 16 targets for delivery by 2010, explicitly recognizes that plants are an essential resource for human well-being. One of its objectives is "to support the development of livelihoods based on sustainable use of plants, and promote the fair and equitable sharing of benefits arising from the use of plant diversity".

There are many practical examples of how botanic gardens are contributing to human well-being. The Jardin Botanique du site Orstom, in the Democratic Republic of Congo, is researching the domestication of useful species for local cultivation. This will allow local communities more easily to meet their needs for healthcare and food, whilst protecting forests that would otherwise be destroyed in attempts to meet these basic needs. The Jardín EtnoBotánico Earth, (at Earth University, Costa Rica) focuses on the conservation of medicinal plants, investigates the potential uses of plants, and communicates this information to local communities. The Tropical Botanic Garden & Research Institute (TBGRI) in Kerala, India, recently ran a project to promote the use of plants for self-sufficiency in basic healthcare. Based on careful research into the healthcare needs and socio-economic situation of four villages in the Thiruvananthapuram District, a TBGRI team made up of botanists, Ayurvedic experts and sociologists worked with villagers to identify and cultivate medicinal plants. The team trained villagers in the preparation of compound drugs for home remedies to treat problems as diverse as burns, sprains and diarrhoea. The project was so successful that other villages asked to become involved, and eventually over 800 families were helped. This type of project is a model that can be developed elsewhere using the skills and resources of local botanic gardens.

Calicut University Botanic Garden, also in Kerala, in its efforts to improve the livelihoods of local poor people

Photo: BGCI

OPPOSITE: The Arturo E. Ragonese Botanic Garden in Argentina is currently being restored.

Plants collected from the wild are of immense importance for healthcare in many parts of the world. In Vietnam, for example, the Dzao people are skilled in the use of a wide range of medicinal plants.

is working to conserve Indian Zingiberaceae, the economically important ginger family. This project has given women a significant role in the sustainable use of their local natural resources, and also established ex-situ conservation measures for the ginger species. The women were taught about the potential of home gardens, trained in nursery development, maintenance and management, and were provided with saplings of medicinal plants to grow in their gardens. They were also given training on the extraction of Travancore starch from the rhizomes of Wild Turmeric (*Curcuma aeruginosa*), which grows abundantly in the area as a wild herb. This plant has a long tradition of use. The starch is used in health drinks and Ayurvedic medicines: for example, hot water extracts of the dried rhizome can be taken orally to reduce inflammation, and it is also classified as a *rasayana* herb, used to counteract ageing processes. Its products are normally quite expensive, so women who collect it from the wild have the opportunity to significantly improve their incomes.

Botanic gardens in major cities are important refuges for wildlife such as these fruit bats in the Royal Botanic Gardens, Sydney.

Photo: Tony Kirkham/Board of the Trustees of the Royal Botanic Gardens, Kew

Nearly 60 per cent of the urban population of Bogotá, Colombia, live below the poverty line. This situation was tackled by a two-year initiative by the Jardín Botánico José Celestino Mutis in Bogotá, in which garden staff worked with deprived local communities to teach them how to grow plants for food. The results were so successful that the President of Colombia and the mayor of Bogotá are supporting a much bigger project by the Colombian Botanic Gardens Network. This project aims to help 6,000 poor urban families in the Ciudad Bolívar suburb to cultivate food plants in home gardens and community areas. Growing their own food will help give these families improved food security, and should go some way to alleviate poverty.

Plants provide essential resources for agriculture, forestry and healthcare. They also provide a wide range of ecological services that are often overlooked or taken for granted. Botanic gardens have a major role to play in conserving the world's plant species, especially those that are under threat of extinction. But they cannot do this alone. The need for joined-up action to save the world's floral diversity has become increasingly recognized in recent years, and in response to this a Global Partnership for Plant Conservation has been formed. The main purpose of this is to support the worldwide implementation of the Global Strategy for Plant Conservation, helping national governments to achieve the 16 ambitious targets of the Strategy by 2010 (see page 151).

The Global Partnership brings together botanic gardens, coordinated by BGCI, with other plant conservation agencies to garner international support for the GSPC. With this harmonized approach some of the targets are likely to be met, including Target 1, which calls for a complete list of the world's flora, and Target 2, which calls for a preliminary assessment of the conservation status of all plants. Other targets will be more demanding, particularly those calling for sustainable production on farmland and restoration of threatened species in their natural habitats. The biggest challenge of all, however, will be how to conserve plants in the face of global climate change.

# RESPONDING TO CLIMATE CHANGE

Global warming is now accepted as an unavoidable fact, with worldwide temperature increases of 0.6°C recorded over the past 40 years and predicted to rise by up to 6°C during the present century. The implications for life on earth are profound. Melting ice caps will cause rising sea levels and the loss of coastal areas of land; terrestrial ecosystems will cease to function in their present form and millions more people will be at risk of hunger as agricultural production systems are radically altered. Plant species provide the basis for all life on earth but many will be unable to adapt to the predicted temperature increases. Models have predicted that plant species will need to migrate, on average, seven to ten miles towards the poles or between eight and sixty metres to areas of higher altitude, every ten years, to cope with current warming. These migration rates are greater than the migration of trees that took place in temperate regions at the end of ice ages in the past. Faced with the onslaught of threats that plant species are already experiencing, extinction for many species appears unavoidable. Botanic gardens are thus likely to play an increasingly crucial role in plant conservation, particularly for those species for which protection in their natural habitats is no longer an option.

Species restricted to specific mountain ranges, for example, will be in trouble as lowland species migrate to higher areas, competing for space with local endemics. Those alpine plants specially adapted to the higher altitudes will face major problems as result of global warming. Reduction in the depth and extent of winter snow cover will potentially greatly increase the severity of temperatures experienced by alpine plants. This aspect of global climate change in the alpine zone is likely to be a critical factor affecting plant survival. Particularly vulnerable alpine areas are ones where the

Photo: Magnus Lidén

mountains are relatively low and the climate is temperate, with little alpine habitat to begin with. Such areas include Greece's Mount Olympus and Spain's Sierra Nevada range, where only 200–400 metres separate timberlines from summits. In Australia, only 11,500 square kilometres of mountain terrain have winter snowfall, and just a fraction of that is true treeless alpine. In neighbouring New Zealand, it has been predicted that a 3°C temperature rise over the next century will wipe out 80 per cent of the country's alpine 'islands', with the extinction of between a third and a half of the 613 alpine plants known there.

Plant conservationists are beginning to plan responses to climate change. In the face of such uncertainty, as many options as possible must be kept available for the future. There is a need for large tracts of natural ecosystems to be conserved and corridors of land established to allow for natural migration. Alongside such protection, ex-situ conservation in botanic gardens, seed banks and arboreta can provide a vital insurance policy to help preserve the maximum range of floral diversity. More immediately, species in areas of particular risk, such as alpine plant species and island floras, need to be rescued now.

Botanic gardens also have a potentially important role to play in helping with adaptation to climate change. The trialling and acclimatization of useful plants – an important role in the past – may once more come to the fore as the climatic ranges for growing crops begin to shift and flowering and fruiting patterns change.

Since their earliest origins in Renaissance Europe, the great botanic gardens of the world have played a central role in scientific discovery and human development. As places of interest and beauty they continue to provide pleasure for the millions of people who visit them. But as the 21st century advances, the behind-the-scenes work of the world's botanic gardens has never been more important. Aimed at securing the future of thousands of plant species, these gardens hold the key to a sustainable future for ourselves and our planet.

OPPOSITE: Alpine plants, a popular feature of botanic gardens, are already feeling the impact of climate change in their natural habitats.

LEFT: Children learn about the value of plants and the need for plant conservation – holding out hope for the future. Cibodas Botanic Garden, Indonesia.

Photo: BGCI

# APPENDIX ONE: EXAMPLES OF PLANTS EXTINCT IN THE WILD BUT SAFE IN CULTIVATION

## SPECIES AND FORMER DISTRIBUTION

*Acanthocladium dockeri* Australia
*Allium sergei* Kazakhstan
*Betula szaferia* Poland
*Bromus bromoideus* France; Belgium
*Bromus interruptus* United Kingdom
*Centaurea leucophaea* subsp. *brunnescens* France
*Clermontia peleana* US (Hawaii)
*Cochlearia polonica* Poland
*Coincya pseuderucastrum* subsp. *puberula* Spain
*Cosmos atrosanguineus* Mexico
*Crataegus harbisonii* US (Alabama, Georgia, Tennessee)
*Cryosophila williamsii* Honduras
*Cyanea pinnatifida* US (Hawaii)
*Cyanea shipmanii* US (Hawaii)
*Cyanea superba* subsp. *superba* US (Hawaii)
*Dendrobium aurantiacum* Bangladesh; Bhutan
*Deppea splendens* Mexico
*Deyeuxia drummondii* Australia

*Diplotaxis siettiana* Spain
*Dypsis acaulis* Madagascar
*Dypsis ceracea* Madagascar
*Franklinia alatamaha* US (Georgia)
*Hemiandra rutilans* Australia
*Hibiscadelphus giffardianus* US (Hawaii)
*Hibiscadelphus hualalaiensis* US (Hawaii)
*Hibiscus storckii* Fiji
*Hopea foxworthyi* Philippines
*Impatiens anaimudica* India (Kerala)
*Kokia cookie* US (Hawaii)
*Laelia gouldiana* Mexico
*Logfia neglecta* Belgium; France (Corsica)
*Lysimachia minoricensis* Spain (Minorca)
*Masdevallia walteri* Costa Rica
*Maytenus lucayana* Bahamas
*Myosotis ruscinonensis* Spain
*Paphiopedilum delenatii* Vietnam
*Penstemon campanulatus* US (New Mexico)
*Platycerium grande* Philippines

*Platycerium grande* var. *tamburinense* Australia (Queensland)
*Polygala antillensis* Martinique
*Polystichum wattii* India (Manipur)
*Pritchardia affinis* US (Hawaii)
*Pritchardia affinis* var. *gracilis* US (Hawaii)
*Pritchardia lowreyana* US (Hawaii)
*Sabal miamiensis* US (Florida)
*Schlumbergera orssichiana* Brazil
*Sisyrinchium macrocarpon* US (Arizona)
*Solanum conocarpum* Puerto Rico; US Virgin Islands
*Sophora toromiro* Rapa Nui (Easter Island)
*Synthyris missurica* subsp. *Stellata* US (Oregon)
*Tecophilaea cyanocrocus* Chile
*Tephrosia angustissima* US (Florida)
*Tulipa sprengeri* Turkey
*Veitchia filifera* Fiji
*Wulfenia baldaccii* Albania

Photo: Ian Oliver/SANBI

# APPENDIX TWO: THE GLOBAL STRATEGY FOR PLANT CONSERVATION

## OBJECTIVES

The ultimate and long-term objective of the Global Strategy for Plant Conservation is to halt the current and continuing loss of plant diversity. The Strategy will provide a framework to facilitate harmony between existing initiatives aimed at plant conservation, to identify gaps where new initiatives are required, and to promote mobilization of the necessary resources.

The Strategy will be a tool to enhance the ecosystem approach to the conservation and sustainable use of biodiversity and focus on the vital role of plants in the structure and functioning of ecological systems and assure provision of the goods and services such systems provide.

## SUB-OBJECTIVES

### A. Understanding and documenting plant diversity

Document the plant diversity of the world, including its use and its distribution in the wild, in protected areas and in ex-situ collections;

Monitor the status and trends in global plant diversity and its conservation, and threats to plant diversity, and identify plant species, plant communities, and associated habitats and ecosystems at risk, including consideration of 'red lists';

Develop an integrated, distributed, interactive information system to manage and make accessible information on plant diversity;

Promote research on the genetic diversity, systematics, taxonomy, ecology and conservation biology of plants and plant communities, and associated habitats and ecosystems, and on social, cultural and economic factors that impact biodiversity, so that plant diversity, both in the wild and in the context of human activities, can be well understood and utilized to support conservation action.

### B. Conserving plant diversity

Improve long-term conservation, management and restoration of plant diversity, plant communities, and the associated habitats and ecosystems, in situ (both in more natural and in more managed environments), and, where necessary to complement in-situ measures, ex situ, preferably in the country of origin. The Strategy will pay special attention to the conservation of the world's important areas of plant diversity, and to the conservation of plant species of direct importance to human societies;

Using plant diversity sustainably:

Strengthen measures to control unsustainable utilization of plant resources;

Support the development of livelihoods based on sustainable use of plants, and promote the fair and equitable sharing of benefits arising from the use of plant diversity.

ABOVE: Herbarium at Antsokay, Madagascar.
OPPOSITE: *Aloe dichotoma* in the Karoo Desert Botanic Garden.

Photo: A. Petignat/Arboretum d'Antsokay

### C. Promoting education and awareness about plant diversity

Articulate and emphasize the importance of plant diversity, the goods and services that it provides, and the need for its conservation and sustainable use, in order to mobilize necessary popular and political support for its conservation and sustainable use;

Building capacity for the conservation of plant diversity:

Enhance the human resources, physical and technological infrastructure necessary, and necessary financial support for plant conservation;

Link and integrate actors to maximize action and potential synergies in support of plant conservation.

## TARGETS OF THE GSPC AND THEIR RATIONALE

### A. Understanding and documenting plant diversity

*Target 1: A widely accessible working list of known plant species, as a step towards a complete world flora*

A working list of known plant species is considered to be a fundamental requirement for plant conservation. The target is considered to be attainable by 2010, especially given that it is to be a working rather than a definitive list, and limited to known organisms (currently about 270,000, which may increase by 10–20% by 2010). Some 900,000 scientific names are known for these 270,000 species. In effect the target will require the compilation and synthesis of existing knowledge, focusing on names and synonyms, and geographical distribution. Both national flora and compilations and international initiatives are important in this respect. The list could be made accessible through the World Wide Web,

complemented by CD-ROM and printed versions. Further work on national and regional floras is necessary to lay the basis for the longer-term aim of developing a complete world flora, including local and vernacular names.

*Target 2: A preliminary assessment of the conservation status of all known plant species, at national, regional and international levels*

Over 60,000 species have been evaluated for conservation status according to internationally accepted criteria, of which 34,000 are classified as globally threatened with extinction (IUCN, 1997). In addition, many countries have assessed the conservation status of their own floras. There are currently about 270,000 known species. Of those still to be evaluated, sufficient information for a full assessment is only available for a proportion. Thus, only a preliminary assessment will have been carried out on the remaining, 'data-deficient' species. Subsequently, further fieldwork will be essential to enable more comprehensive assessments to be undertaken.

*Target 3: Development of models with protocols for plant conservation and sustainable use, based on research and practical experience*

Conservation biology research, and methodologies and practical techniques for conservation are fundamental to the conservation of plant diversity and the sustainable use of its components. These can be applied through the development and effective dissemination of relevant models and protocols for applying best practice, based on the results of existing and new research and practical experience of management. 'Protocols' in this sense can be understood as practical guidance on how to conduct plant conservation and sustainable use activities in particular settings. Key areas where the development of models with protocols is required include: the integration of in-situ and ex-situ conservation; maintenance of threatened plants within ecosystems; applying the ecosystem approach; balancing sustainable use with conservation; and methodologies for setting conservation priorities; and methodologies for monitoring conservation and sustainable use activities.

### B. Conserving plant diversity

*Target 4: At least 10 per cent of each of the world's ecological regions effectively conserved*

About 10 per cent of the land surface is currently covered by protected areas. In general, forests and mountain areas are well represented in protected areas, while natural grasslands (such as prairies) and coastal and estuarine ecosystems, including mangroves, are poorly represented. The target would imply: (i) increasing the representation of different ecological regions in protected areas, and (ii) increasing the effectiveness of protected areas. Since some ecological regions will include protected areas covering more than 10 per cent of their area, the qualifier "at least" is used. In some cases, ecosystems restoration and rehabilitation may be necessary. Effective conservation is understood to mean that the area is managed to achieve a favorable conservation status for plant species and communities. Various approaches are available for use in the identification of ecological regions, based on major vegetation types. Further targets may be agreed in the future.

*Target 5: Protection of 50 per cent of the most important areas for plant diversity assured*
The most important areas for plant diversity would be identified according to the criteria including endemism, species richness, and/or uniqueness of habitats, including relict ecosystems, also taking into account the provision of ecosystem services. They would be identified primarily at local and national levels. Protection would be assured through effective conservation measures, including protected areas. Experience from regional initiatives on important plant areas, as well as a similar approach on important bird areas, suggests that 50 per cent is a realistic target for 2010. In the longer term the protection of all important plant areas should be assured.

### Target 6: At least 30 per cent of production lands managed consistent with the conservation of plant diversity
1. For the purpose of the target, production lands refer to lands where the primary purpose is agriculture (including horticulture), grazing, or wood production. Consistent with conservation of plant diversity implies that a number of objectives are integrated into the management of such production lands:
   Conservation of plant diversity, which is an integral part of the production system itself (ie, crop, pasture or tree species and genetic diversity);
   Protection of other plant species in the production landscape that are unique, threatened, or of particular socio-economic value;
   Use of management practices that avoid significant adverse impacts on plant diversity in surrounding ecosystems, for example by avoiding excessive release of agro-chemicals and preventing unsustainable soil erosion.

2. Increasingly, integrated production methods are being applied in agriculture, including integrated pest management, conservation agriculture, and on-farm management of plant genetic resources. Similarly, sustainable forest management practices are being more broadly applied. Against this background, and with the above understanding of the terms used, the target is considered feasible. Higher targets are appropriate for natural or semi-natural forests and grasslands.

### Target 7: 60 per cent of the world's threatened species conserved in situ
Conserved in situ is here understood to mean that populations of the species are effectively maintained in at least one protected area or through other in-situ management measures. In some countries this figure has already been met, but it would require additional efforts in many countries. The target should be seen as a step towards the effective in-situ conservation of all threatened species

*Target 8: 60 per cent of threatened plant species in accessible ex-situ collections, preferably in the country of origin, and 10 per cent of them included in recovery and restoration programmes*
Currently, over 10,000 threatened species are maintained in living collections (botanic gardens, seed banks, and tissue culture collections), representing some 30 per cent of known threatened species. It is considered that this could be increased to meet the proposed target by 2010, with additional resources, technology development and transfer, especially for species with recalcitrant seeds. Within this target it is suggested that priority be given to critically endangered species, for which a target of 90 per cent should be attained. It is estimated that currently about 2 per cent of threatened species are included in recovery and restoration programmes. Against this baseline, a target of 10 per cent is recommended.

*Target 9: 70 per cent of the genetic diversity of crops and other major socio-economically valuable plant species conserved, and associated indigenous and local knowledge maintained*
Theory and practice demonstrate that, with an appropriate strategy, 70 per cent of the genetic diversity of a crop can be contained in a relatively small sample (generally, less than one thousand accessions). For any one species, therefore, the target is readily attainable. For some 200–300 crops, it is expected that 70 per cent of genetic diversity is already conserved ex situ in gene banks. Genetic diversity is also conserved through on-farm management. By working with local communities, associated indigenous and local knowledge can also be maintained. Combining gene bank, on-farm, and other in-situ approaches, the target could be reached for all crops in production, as well as major forage and tree species. Other major socio-economically important species, such as medicinal plants, could be selected on a case-by-case basis, according to national priorities. Through the combined actions of countries, some 2,000 or 3,000 species could be covered in all.

*Target 10: Management plans in place for at least 100 major alien species that threaten plants, plant communities and associated habitats and ecosystems*
There is no agreed reliable estimate of the number of alien species that threaten indigenous plants, plant communities and associated habitats and ecosystems to such an extent that they may be considered as "major". It is recommended, therefore, that the target be established for an absolute number of such major invasive alien species. The wording "at least 100" is considered appropriate. The 100 invasive alien species would be selected on the basis of national priorities, also taking into account their significance at regional and global levels. For many alien species, it is expected that different management plans will be required in different countries in which they threaten plants, plant communities and associated habitats and ecosystems. This target would be considered as a first step towards developing management plans for all major alien species that threaten plants, plant communities and associated habitats and ecosystems.

## C. Using plant diversity sustainably

*Target 11: No species of wild flora endangered by international trade*
The proposed formulation of the target is more precise since it focuses on those species that are actually threatened by international trade. So formulated, the target is attainable and is complementary to target 12. Species of wild flora endangered by international trade include but are not limited to species listed on CITES appendix 1. The target is consistent with the main purpose of the CITES Strategic Plan (to 2005): "No species of wild flora subject to unsustainable exploitation because of international trade".

*Target 12: 30 per cent of plant-based products derived from sources that are sustainably managed*
1. Plant-based products include food products, timber, paper and other wood-based products, other fibre products, and ornamental, medicinal and other plants for direct use.

2. Sources that are sustainably managed are understood to include: natural or semi-natural ecosystems that are sustainably managed (by avoiding over-harvesting of products, or damage to other components of the ecosystem), excepting that commercial extraction of resources from some primary forests and near-pristine ecosystems of important conservation value might be excluded; sustainably managed, plantation forests and agricultural lands.

3. In both cases, sustainable management should be understood to integrate social and environmental considerations, such as the fair and equitable sharing of benefits and the participation of indigenous and local communities.

4. Indicators for progress might include: direct measures, eg products meeting relevant verified standards (such as for organic food, certified timber, and intermediate standards that codify good practices for sustainable agriculture and forestry); indirect measures, eg products from sources considered to be sustainable, or near-sustainable, on the basis of farming system analyses, taking into account the adoption of integrated production methods. Assessment of progress will be assisted by the development of criteria and indicators of sustainable agricultural and forest management.
5. Certified organic foods and timber currently account for about 2 per cent of production globally. For several product categories, examples exist of 10–20 per cent of products meeting intermediate standards. Against this baseline, the target is considered to be attainable. It would be applied to each category of plant-based products, understanding that for some categories it will be more difficult to reach and more difficult to monitor progress. Implementation would require a combination of product-specific and sector-wide approaches, consistent with the Convention's programme of work on agricultural biodiversity.

**Target 13: The decline of plant resources, and associated indigenous and local knowledge innovations and practices which support sustainable livelihoods, local food security and health care, halted**

Plant diversity underpins livelihoods, food security and health care. This target is consistent with one of the widely agreed international development targets, namely to "ensure that current trends in the loss of environmental resources are effectively reversed at both global and national levels by 2015". It is recommended feasible to halt the decline by 2010 and subsequently to reverse the decline. Relevant plant resources and methods to address their decline are largely site specific and thus implementation must be locally driven. The scope of the target is understood to encompass plant resources and associated ethnobotanical knowledge. Measures to address the decline in associated indigenous and local knowledge should be implemented consistent with the Convention's programme of work on Article 8(j) and related provisions.

### D. Promoting education and awareness about plant diversity

**Target 14: The importance of plant diversity and the need for its conservation incorporated into communication, education and public awareness programmes**

Communication, education and the raising of public awareness about the importance of plant diversity are crucial for the achievement of all the targets of the strategy. This target is understood to refer to both informal and formal education at all levels, including primary, secondary and tertiary education. Key target audiences include not only children and other students, but also policy-makers and the public in general. Consideration should be given to developing specific indicators to monitor progress towards achievement of the overall target. It may be helpful to develop indicators for specific target audiences. Given the strategic importance of education about plant

Photo: A. Petignat/Arboretum d'Antsokay

*Alluaudiopsis marnieriana,* Madagascar.

conservation, this issue should be included not only in environmental curricula, but should also be included in broader areas of mainstream education policy.

### E. Building capacity for the conservation of plant diversity

**Target 15: The number of trained people working with appropriate facilities in plant conservation increased, according to national needs, to achieve the targets of this Strategy**

The achievement of the targets included in the Strategy will require very considerable capacity-building, particularly to address the need for conservation practitioners trained in a range of disciplines, with access to adequate facilities. In addition to training programmes, the achievement

of this target will require long-term commitment to maintaining infrastructure. "Appropriate facilities" are understood to include adequate technological, institutional and financial resources. Capacity-building should be based on national needs assessments. It is likely that the number of trained people working in plant conservation worldwide will need to double by 2010. Given the current geographical disparity between biodiversity and expertise, this is likely to involve considerably more than a doubling of capacity in many developing countries, small island developing States, and countries with economies in transition. Increased capacity should be understood to include not only in-service training, but also the training of additional staff and other stakeholders, particularly at the community level.

**Target 16: Networks for plant conservation activities established or strengthened at national, regional and international levels**

Networks can enhance communication and provide a mechanism for the exchange of information, know-how and technology. Networks will provide an important component in the coordination of effort among many stakeholders for the achievement of all the targets of the strategy. They will also help to avoid duplication of effort and to optimize the efficient allocation of resources. Effective networks provide a means to develop common approaches to plant conservation problems, to share policies and priorities and to help disseminate the implementation of all such policies at different levels. They can also help to strengthen links between different sectors relevant to conservation, eg the botanical, environmental, agricultural, forest and educational sectors. Networks provide an essential link between on-the-ground conservation action and coordination, monitoring and policy development at all levels. This target is understood to include the broadening of participation in existing networks, as well as the establishment, where necessary, of new networks.

# USEFUL ADDRESSES

## INTERNATIONAL

**Botanic Gardens Conservation International (BGCI)**
Descanso House
199 Kew Road
Richmond
Surrey
TW9 3BW
UK
Tel: +44 (0)20 8332 5953
Fax: +44 (0)20 8332 5956
Email: info@bgci.org
http://www.bgci.org

**Botanic Garden Education Network (BGEN)**
Royal Botanic Gardens
Kew
Richmond
Surrey
TW9 3AB
UK

**Convention on Biological Diversity (CBD)**
413 Saint Jacques Street, suite 800
Montreal, Quebec, Canada
H2Y 1N9
Tel: +1 514 288 2220
Fax: +1 514 288 6588
http://www.biodiv.org
Email: secretariat@biodiv.org

**Convention on International Trade in Endangered Species of Wild Fauna and Flora (CITES)**
CITES Secretariat
International Environment House
Chemin des Anémones
CH–1219 Châtelaine, Geneva
Switzerland
Tel: +41 22 917 8139/40
Fax: +41 22 797 3417
Email: cites@unep.ch
http://www.cites.org

**Fauna & Flora International**
Great Eastern House
Tenison Road
Cambridge
CB1 2TT
UK
Tel: + 44 (0) 1223 571000
Fax: + 44 (0) 1223 461481
Email: info@fauna-flora.org
http://www.fauna-flora.org

**Plantlife International**
14 Rollestone Street
Salisbury
Wiltshire
SP1 1DX
UK
Tel: +44 (0)1722 342730
Fax: +44 (0)1722 329035
Email: enquiries@plantlife.org.uk
http://www.plantlife.org.uk/

**The World Conservation Union (IUCN)**
Rue Mauverney 28
Gland
1196
Switzerland
Tel: +41 22 999 0000
Fax: +41 22 999 0002
Email: webmaster@iucn.org
http://www.iucn.org

**United Nations Environment Programme World Conservation Monitoring Centre (UNEP-WCMC)**
219 Huntingdon Road, Cambridge CB3 0DL, UK
Tel: +44 (0)1223 277314 Fax: +44 (0)1223 277136
Email: info@unep-wcmc.org
http://www.unep-wcmc.org/

## EUROPE

**European Botanic Gardens Consortium**
c/o Botanic Gardens Conservation International,
Descanso House,
199 Kew Road,
Richmond,
Surrey,
TW9 3BW

**Arbeitsgemeinschaft Österreichischer Botanischer Gärten**
Institut für Botanik und Botanischer Garten
Universität Wien
Rennweg 14
A-1030 WIEN
Austria
http://www.botanik.univie.ac.at/hbv/deutsch/ag_oebg/oebotgar.htm

**Belarus Botanic Garden Association**
Central Botanical Garden,
National Academy of Sciences,
Surganova Street 2v,
220012 Minsk,
Belarus

**Vereiniging Botanische Tuinenen Arboreta (VBTA)**
(Association des Jardins Botaniques et Arboreta de Belgique)
Jardin Botanique National de Belgique/Nationale Plantentuin van Belgie
Domaine de Bouchout
B-1860 Meise
Belgium

**Czech Botanic Gardens Union**
Prague Botanical Garden
Nadvorni 134
171 00 Prague 7 – Troja
Czech Republic

**Baltic Botanic Gardens Association**
Kaunas Botanical Garden
Vytautas Magnus University
Zilibero Str 6
LT–46324 KAUNAS
Lithuania

**National Botanic Garden Network of Finland**
Helsinki Universtiy Botanic Garden
PO Box 44
FI-00014 University of Helsinki
Helsinki
Finland
Tel: +358 50 548 7692

**Jardins Botaniques de France et des Pays Francophones (JBF)**
Museum National d'Histoire Naturelle (Jardin des Plantes)
Bibliotheque Central
38, rue Geoffroy Saint-Hilaire
F–75005
Paris
France
http://www.bgci.org/JBF_fr/

**Association of Georgian Botanic Gardens, Dendraria and Historic Parks**
Central (Tbilisi) Botanic Garden
0105 Tbilisi
Botanikuri 1
Georgia
Tel: +995 32 72 11 85
Fax: +995 32 72 34 09

**Verband Botanischer Garten e.V.**
Lehrstuhl Spezielle Botanik und Botanischer Garten
Postfach 102148, Ruhr-Universitat
Universitatstrasse 150
D–44801 Bochum
Germany
http://www.biologie.uni-ulm.de/verband/

**Association of Hungarian Arboreta and Botanical Gardens**
Corvinus University of Budapest
Faculty of Horticultural Science, Dept of Floriculture and Dendrology
Villányi str. 35–43
H-1118 Budapest
Hungary

**Gruppo di Lavoro per gli Orti Botanici et i Giardini Storici dell Società Botanica Italiana**
Orto Botanico dell'Università
Viale Caduti in Guerra 127
I–41100 Modena
Italy
Tel: +39 0592056011
Fax: +39 0592056005
http://www.societabotanicaitaliana.it/laygruppo.asp?IDSezione=20

**Baltic Botanic Gardens Association**
Kaunas Botanical Garden
Vytautas Magnus University
Zilibero Str 6
LT–46324 KAUNAS
Lithuania

Dutch Botanic Garden Association
Utrecht University Botanic Gardens
PO Box 80162
NL–3508 TD Utrecht
The Netherlands
Tel: +31 (0)30 253 2876
Fax: + 31 (0)30 253 5177

Polish Botanic Gardens Association
Ogród Botaniczny UW
Warsaw University Botanic Garden
Aleje Ujazdowskie 4
00–478 Warszawa
Poland
+ 48 22 628 7514
+ 48 22 622 6446

Rada Ogrodów Botanicznych w Polsce
Ogród Botaniczny - Centrum Zachowania
Róznorodnosci Biologicznej
Polskiej Akademii Nauk
Powsin, P.O. Box 45
ul. Prawdziwka 2
02–937 WARSAW 76
Poland

Associaçâo Ibero-Macaronésica de Jardins
Botânicos
c/o Instituto Superior de Agronomia
Universida de Tecnica de Lisboa
Jardim Botanico da Ajuda
Calcada da Ajuda s/n 1300–011
Lisboa
Portugal

Association of Romanian Botanical Gardens
Faculty of Biology, University of Bucharest
Soseaua Cotroceni 32
Sector 6, OP 35 Cod 76258
Bucharesti
Romania

Council of Botanic Gardens of Russia
Main Botanical Gardens RAS
4 Botanischeskaya Street
127276 Moscow
Russia

Asociación Ibero-Macaronésica de Jardines
Botánicos
Réal Jardin Botánico
Juan Carlos I
Campus de la Universidad de Alcalá
28805 Alcalá de Henares
Spain
http://www.aimjb.org

International Association of Botanic Gardens
(IABG), Spain
Jardín Botánico de Córdoba
Avda de Linneo, s/n
E–14004 Córdoba
Spain
Tel: +34 957 203154
Fax: +34 957 295333
Email: jardinbotcord@retemail.es

Council of Botanical Gardens of Ukraine
M.M. Grishko Central Botanical Garden
Timiryazevskaya Street 1
01014 KIEV
Ukraine
Tel: +38 044 295 4105/0866
Fax: +38 044 296 2649

PlantNetwork – The Plant Collections Network of
Britain and Ireland
c/o University Computing Service
New Museums Site
Pembroke Street
Cambridge
CB2 3QH
UK
Tel: +44 (0)1223 763901
Fax: +44 (0)1223 763901
www.plantnetwork.org

Royal Horticultural Society (RHS)
80 Vincent Square
London
SW1P 2PE
UK
Tel: +44 (0)20 7834 4333
Email: info@rhs.org.uk
http://www.rhs.org.uk

# NORTH AMERICA
## Canadian Botanical Conservation Network (CBCN)
Royal Botanical Gardens
P.O. Box 399
Hamilton
Ontario L8N 3H8
Canada
Tel: +1 416 527 1158
Fax: +1 416 577 0375
http://www.rbg.ca/cbcn/
Email: cbcn@rbg.ca

American Public Gardens Network (APGA)
100 W 10th St, Suite 614
Wilmington
DE 19801
USA
Tel: +1 302 655 7100, ext 16
Fax: +1 302 655 8100
http://www.aabga.org/
Email: info@aabga.org

Centre for Plant Conservation (CPC)
P.O. Box 299
St. Louis
MO 63166–0299
USA
Tel: +1 314 577 9450
Fax: +1 314 577 9465
Email: cpc@mobot.org
http://www.centerforplantconservation.org/

# LATIN AMERICA & CARIBBEAN
## Asociación Latinoamericana y del Caribe de Jardines Botánicos (ALCJB)
Quindío Botanic Garden
AA 123
Armenia
Colombia

Red de Etnojardines Hermanos Latinoamericanos
c/o Center for Latin American and Caribbean
Studies
University of Georgia
290 S. Hull Street
Athens,
GA 3060
USA
Tel: +1 706 583 0619
Fax: +1 706 542 8432

Caribbean Botanic Gardens for Conservation
Network (CBGCN)
C/o Belize Botanic Gardens
PO Box 180
San Ignacio
Cayo
Belice
Central America
Tel: +501 824 3101
Fax: +501 824 3301
Email: info@belizebotanic.org

Red Argentina de Jardines Botánicos
Jardin Botánico "Arturo E. Raginese"
Instituto de Recursos Biológicos
CRN–CNIA–INTA
Las Cabañas y De Los Reseros s.n.
(B1712WAA) Castelar
Buenos Aires
Argentina
Tel: +54 (0) 11 4621 1819 /4621 0840
Fax: +54 (0) 11 4481 2360 /4621 6903
Email: ana@cirn.inta.gov.ar

Rede Brasileira de Jardins Botânicos (RBJB)
c/o Dr Tânia Sampaio Pereira
Jardim Botanico do Rio de Janeiro Rua
Pacheco Leao 915
22460 030
Rio de Janeiro
Brazil
Tel: +55 021 294 6590/51
Fax: +55 021 259 5041
http://www.rbjb.org.br/

Red Nacional de Jardines Botánicos de Colombia
Quindío Botanic Garden
AA 123
Armenia
Colombia
Tel: +57 (9) 67 1210 1788
Fax: +57 (9) 67 1217 8859
www.humboldt.org.co/jardinesdecolombia

Red Nacional de Jardines Botánicos de Cuba
Jardín Botánico Nacional de Cuba
Universidad de la Habana
Carretera del Rocio, Km 3.5 Calabazar
Boyeros,
Ciudad de Habana
Cuba
Tel: +53 7 44 5525
Fax: +53 7 32 8722
Email: hajb@ceniai.inf.cu

Red Nacional de Jardines Botánicos del Ecuador
c/o Jardín Botánico de Quito
Fundación Botánica de Los Andes

PO Box 17–21–1640
Quito
Ecuador
www.jardinesbotanicosecuador.com

**Asociación Mexicana de Jardines Botánicos (AMJB)**
Jardín Botánico Regional
Centro de Investigación Científica de Yucatán AC
Calle 43 No 130 Col Chuburná de Hidalgo
CP 97200, AP 87 Cordemex
Mérida, Yucatán
Mexico
Tel: +52 999 9813914 /9813923 /9813966
Fax: +52 999 9813900
Email: ambj@ecologia.edu.mx
http://www.ecologia.edu.mx/amjb/

## INDIA
**Indian Botanic Garden Network (IBGN)**
National Botanical Research Institue
Rana Pratap Marg
Lucknow 226001
India
http://www.ibgn.org

## REGIONAL: AFRICA
**African Botanic Gardens Network (ABGN)**
ABGN is divided into 6 regions, and each region is
represented by a focal point on the ABGN steering
Committee along with the ABGN Coordinator:
please check the website for the contact details of
the coordinator and focal points.
c/o Durban Botanic Gardens
PO Box 3740
Durban 4000
KwaZulu-Natal
South Africa
Tel: +27 31 2011303
Fax: +27 31 2017382
http://www.bgci.org/africa/abgn/
Email: africa@bgci.org

**Central African Botanic Gardens and Arboreta Network (CABGAN)**
c/o Limbe Botanic Garden
P.O.Box 437
Limbe
Cameroon
Tel: +237 333 2620

Fax/Tel: +237 999 89 13
Email: lbzg@bifunde.com

**South African National Biodiversity Institute (SANBI)**
Private Bag X101
Pretoria 0001
South Africa
www.sanbi.org

## SOUTH-EAST ASIA
**Indonesian Network for Plant Conservation (INetPC)**
Kebun Raya Bogor
Jalan Ir. H. Juanda No 13 PO Box 309
BOGOR 16003
Indonesia
Tel: +62 251 336 935
Fax: +62 251 322 187
Email: inetpc@indo.net.id
www.bogor.indo.net.id/inetpc

**Japan Association of Botanical Gardens**
Tea Heim Asaka Bld 201
1-15-11, Tabata, Kita-ku
Tokyo
14-0014
Japan
Tel: +81 (0)3 5685 1431
Fax: +81(0)3 5685 1453
Email: nsk@fancy.ocn.ne.jp
www.syokubutsuen-kyokai.jp

**Korean Association of Botanic Gardens and Arboreta (KABGA)**
c/ The Arboretum, College of Agriculture and Life
Sciences
Seoul National University
103 Seodun-dong
SUWEON 441-744
Korea
Tel: +82 31 290 2328/2338
Fax: + 82 331 293 1797

## CHINA
**Botanical Garden Conservation Branch, Society of Environmental Sciences of China**
Nanjing Botanical Garden
Mem. Sun Yat-sen, PO Box 1435
NANJING 210014
Jiangsu Province, China

**Chinese Academy of Sciences**
52 Sanlihe Road
Beijing 100864
China
Tel: +86 (0) 1068597289
Fax: +86 (0) 1068512458
www.cashg.ac.cn

**International Association of Botanic Gardens (IABG), China**
Nanjing Botanic Garden, Mem Sun Yat-Sen,
Institute of Botany, Jiangsu Province and
Chinese Academy of Sciences
PO Box 1435 Nanjing
Jiangsu 210014
China
Tel: +86 25 4432075
Fax: +86 25 4432074
jsszzzzz@public1.ptt.jsc.cn

## AUSTRALASIA
**Australian Network for Plant Conservation (ANPC)**
GPO Box 1777
CANBERRA CITY
ACT 2601
Australia
Tel: +61 (0)2 6250 9450
Fax: +61 (0)2 6250 9599
www.anbg.gov.au/anpc

**Botanical Gardens of Australia and New Zealand (BGANZ)**
GPO Box 1777
Canberra ACT 2601
Australia
http://www.anbg.gov.au/chabg/

**New Zealand Plant Conservation Network**
Wellington City Council
PO Box 2199
Wellington
New Zealand
Tel: +64 (0)4 801 3627
Fax: +64 (0)4 801 3074
http://www.nzpcn.org.nz

# INDEX

# ACKNOWLEDGEMENTS

Many people have contributed ideas, suggestions and information for this book and I am grateful to them all. Particular thanks are due to Fiona Wild, who helped with research on botanic gardens of Europe and North America, and to Kerry Waylen who compiled background information on various botanic gardens and prepared the annexes. Kerry Waylen and Jemima Taylor provided valuable help with picture research for the book. Suzanne Sharrock, Mark Richardson, Douglas Gibbs and Etelka Leadlay have suggested sources of information and shared their extensive knowledge of botanic gardens with me. David Galbraith prepared a history of the Royal Botanic Garden, Hamilton with assistance from David Butler, Barb McKean and Ann Milovsoroff. Kay Havens, Margaret Johnson, Adil Guner, Nikita Mergelov, Professor Chin See Chung, Kingsley Dixon, Jenny Rowntree, Stephen Forbes, David Frodin and Christopher Willis all kindly provided information for the text. The experience and expertise of Peter Wyse Jackson, Secretary General of BGCI from 1994–2005, has influenced the book in many ways, for which I am most grateful.

David Rae very generously made available a copy of his PhD thesis *Botanic gardens and their live plant collections: present and future roles*. This has been an invaluable reference source for the book, particularly for historical aspects of botanic garden develop-ment. The hospitality provided by all the gardens I have visited over the past two years has been outstanding. I am particularly grateful to Professor Peter and Dr Pat Raven of the Missouri Botanic Garden.

The generosity of botanic gardens that have made photographs freely available for use by BGCI in the preparation of this book is gratefully acknowledged. Particular thanks are given to the Royal Botanic Gardens, Kew, who provided a particularly large number of images from around the world. The individuals credited alongside photographs in the book are all thanked sincerely for providing the images of plants and gardens. BGCI staff members have also made available photographs they have taken as a contribution to BGCI's picture library. Thanks are due to Anle Tieu, Bian Tan, Sarah Dixon, Sarah Kneebone, Mark Richardson and Suzanne Sharrock.

HSBC has supported an extensive programme of work at BGCI through the Investing in Nature Programme for the period of 2002–2007, enabling BGCI to expand its work considerably. This book is one small outcome of this programme, which also supported the development and implementation of the Global Strategy for Plant Conservation, the creation of the Global Partnership for Plant Conservation, and a wide range of conservation and education activities. Thank you.